I AM TALKING ABOUT
YOU

THINGS WE WOULD LIKE TO SAY (AND DON'T)
to friends, family, acquaintances and strangers that annoy us.

WELBOURN EILER

First Stillwater River Publications Edition

ISBN-10: 1-946-30062-4
ISBN-13: 978-1-946-30062-1

1 2 3 4 5 6 7 8 9 10
Written by Welborn Eiler.
Cover design by Nathanael Vinbury

Published by Stillwater River Publications, Pawtucket, RI, USA.

The views and opinions expressed in this book are solely those of the author and do not necessarily reflect the views and opinions of the publisher.

TABLE OF CONTENTS

DRIVING

ETIQUETTE

INAPPROPRIATE OR STRANGE BEHAVIOR

PERSONAL PROBLEMS

SOCIAL CONSCIOUSNESS

INTRODUCTION

How much would you be willing to pay to tell someone off in writing, with absolutely no consequences whatsoever? What would it be worth to you to see their face when they come upon a topic that has their name written all over it. Will they recognize it is them? Will they come to appreciate that you are giddy with excitement with the prospect that they are about to read about something that you have been dying to tell them; that special something that makes you so crazy that you want to put your own eye out. What is it worth to you to cause that special someone to change that one thing they do that makes you a candidate for the loony farm waiting list?

This book is filled with topics that you will want (or even need) to share with a number of people who form your inner and outer circle of life. Once you read a topic that is familiar to you, their name will immediately pop into your head. They frequently do this ridiculous and sometimes awkward, aggravating, or stupid thing, or they always exhibit a specific behavior that you find annoying challenging, and even hurtful. They do it all the time. You have been dying to mention something about it to them, but are too chicken to act. In some cases, it is merely an annoyance; in others, you can feel your fingers curling to mimic wringing someone's neck. When you read that special topic that rings your bell, you will say to yourself, "I don't know how I am going to do it, but they have to see this".

And I have made it possible for you to be able to do just that. Just mail a copy of this book to your victim and, if you have the guts to do it, put a little sticky note on the page or pages where you want to direct their attention. How you send it can be tricky. That all depends upon whether you want them to know it comes from you. You might need to drive a few hundred (or thousand) miles away and then deposit it in a post office box in a state that they will never be able to connect to you (that is what I would do, but I disavow any guidance on planning these types of things). That is not my forte. Telling people off with brutal honesty is more of my specialty. Do not tear out any of the pages. In case you didn't know, that is prohibited by federal law. In case you want to check up on this for accuracy, you will find it as a subsection of the same law that does not allow you to rip the tag off a mattress–The Sealy/Simmons Law of 1881. (Yes, I made that up).

We all make decisions dependent upon priority and value. If you value the great opportunity that this book will create for you, you now have that opportunity. You will create for yourself lifelong pleasure in knowing that one thing that has made your blood boil is finally out there and visible to that special someone; you can finally sleep at night. You will have opened a door that you always saw as an impenetrable vault. You will be able to take great pleasure in knowing that you have created for yourself the potential of, hopefully, opening the eyes of those who have remained clueless for far too long. The opportunity before you is so great that it would have defied logic for you to pass up the opportunity to read the things I say to friends, family members, acquaintances and strangers that annoy you. You should never defy logic. If you have to defy anything, defy gravity. At least you will have something else to talk about besides the huge step you will now be taking to inner peace and contentment. I kind of, sort of, marginally, guarantee it!

I AM TALKING ABOUT YOU!

There are many things that we see or become associated with in our lives that are upsetting, unnerving or aggravating. In some cases, they are pet peeves that make us crazy. In other cases, they are just plain wrong or more than a tad bit bothersome. Most of the time we say nothing because it really isn't worth it. But sometimes the negative effect on us is so great we can barely stand it. We often express our dissatisfaction or frustration internally or after the fact without confronting the source of our discontent. Holding back has obvious advantages. It means that you have avoided a potentially explosive situation. The bombs have gone off inside of you big-time, but you do nothing to express your true feelings or, worse yet, to vent your anger. You have chosen the safest route possible. In some cases, you have said what is on your mind, but your words have fallen on deaf ears.

Sometimes the situation is a fleeting moment that will not likely be repeated. That is especially the case if it involves a stranger that you might never meet again. Sometimes it is a situation that we all deal with that is due to the indifference or disdain of a business or even an entire industry. More often, however, it involves someone you may very well know. It may be a circumstance you have encountered before. This isn't the first time this situation has occurred, and it is unlikely to be the last. In fact, I can guarantee you that you have probably promised yourself, time and again, that the next time it occurs you are going to let the offending person have it. And it does happen again; and you still do nothing. You remain annoyed and stress yourself out with an internal fight about what you should have done and did not do that remains unresolved at the end of the day.

Instead of expressing yourself or letting go in a manner that you might probably dread, here is an alternative you might want to consider. Let someone else (like me) take care of this problem for you. How can I do that? For one thing, I like to write about the feelings you secretly harbor. Instead of you saying anything at all, just let the offending person read what I have written in this book. Tell them it is funny, if they are into that sort of thing. Tell them not to read it, if you want to do some reverse psychology on them. Tell them to read the section immediately before or after the one you want them to focus on, in the hope that their wandering eye will move where you are desperately hoping it might.

You have to be a little proactive if you want to succeed in your mission. This book won't read itself.

Some of things that I have written "cut like a knife". In fact, I have been told that there are some sections that are "too brutal". Good. Nothing could please me more. Why the heck do you think I wrote this in the first place? Because I wanted to sweetly convey messages? Think again. That hasn't worked in the past; no reason to expect it to work now. Some passages are so outrageously hurtful that the target reader may not possibly think they could ever be that bad. They may also be too difficult to read because they hit home and touch a nerve. It is easier to think I am awful and rude, a terrible writer, and the most horrible person on the planet, than it is to be angry at you or anyone else. I am doing you a favor. You're welcome. And when you read some of these topics and what I have to say about them, you will think to yourself, "I think that same thing all the time!" You are also thinking that you wish you could say it but don't have the nerve or guts to do it. I know, that is why I wrote this masterpiece; I am both a writer and a mind-reader.

I do throw in a little humor here and there, so, in this way, there is the potential that a person may be hurt, but still slightly amused. It is that spoonful of sugar that will, hopefully, help someone choke down some much-deserved medicine. This tact just might allow for a glimmer of hope that the reader might see themselves in the act or circumstance I describe and self-correct their behavior (as if that is even possible in some cases). So, the potential is out there that the truth may have no effect, a positive effect, or a very negative effect. But, at the end of the day, does it really matter if there is zero self-correction? At least something you have been dying to say is finally out there for someone else's consideration, amusement or reciprocal annoyance.

I think it is common knowledge that, when you do let someone know how you feel about them or something they did, their first reaction is to be defensive. They really won't listen to you. They can't. It is the same way with a child. They not only will not correct their behavior, they will do it even more in spite. The bottom line is this: people find it very difficult to heed the advice and counsel of people they know. But, for some reason, people will listen to what a perfect stranger may have to say. In reading what I have written, some people may actually see something that ticks them off that they themselves do. They may not see the message as having anything to do with them. They may not connect the dots. It makes no sense, but that is human nature and it is also probably the best reason why people do annoying things; they don't think they are annoying.

My hope and goal in writing about these life annoyances is to cause people to take a good and hard look at themselves and others. The perceptions that people will have in reading what I have written may be directly proportional to the impact I have in calling transgressions to their attention. How do I know, I don't! But it does stand to reason that people who see themselves being harpooned will not be happy and will find it hard to have anything good to say about what I have written. Unless, of course, they think this is the best piece of trashy garbage they have ever read.

My goal in writing this is simple. I want people to see who they really are, and what people are saying about them either under their breath or to others. I am your proxy. I want people to recognize their faults in the form of a great awakening. By taking ownership of one's failings, completely or minimally, a person might be less inclined to take issue with everyone else. If they see a mirror reflection of themselves in a book, they might be less likely to respond in a negative way and they might be willing to take corrective action that, in the eyes of many, is a loooooong time in coming. Seeing oneself in this less confrontational, but in-your-face, way might actually cause a person to be become more tolerant and nicer. They even might possibly be willing to accept some blame for what is clearly and without question gross, stupid, ridiculous and unreasonable conduct. For those who have been the recipients of poor behavior, the change will be a great welcome that may result in the heaping of great praise and gifts. You never know.

When you get right down to it, it is intolerance and the lack of acceptance that really floats my boat, and yours as well. The world is way too full of people who are unwilling to accept responsibility for their actions. "It isn't my fault my car plowed into your house." Your house shouldn't have been there in the first place." It is always someone else's fault. We all hear that a lot. Everyone wants to sue everyone else. They seem to be unable to see their own failures when their culpability is so obviously at play. It makes me crazy! I am sure it does the same thing to you. It bugs me enough so that I felt compelled to write this all down. Maybe seeing it in black and white can change lives, somehow, some way.

I certainly hope that I do not come across as perfect. I am far from it. I might be as far from perfect as you can possibly imagine. I know a number of people you could speak to who could provide affidavits of my inferiority and deep character flaws with very little prompting. And I am not just picking on others. For your information and great pleasure, I do many of the things I describe in this book. What is good for the goose is definitely good for the gander. How the heck do you think I came up with so many of these situations and aggravations? Many of the topics, circumstances, and situations I describe are things that I do, and quite proudly I might add. I am glad I do them, however, because they have given me material for my writing. I have self-reflected on the possibility that, because of my various failings, I might have some serious problems that deserve attention. Not only because I am capable of doing some of these nutty things. More importantly, because I seem to have this burning need to proclaim my disgust for them in the first place. Why else would I feel the need to "let it all out" and express my varying views? Obviously, something is wrong with me; enough so that I felt compelled to talk about myself and others in this fashion. Do I find this all therapeutic? Perhaps, but you certainly have to wonder why I feel the need to express myself in a way that many might consider to be rude and over the top. In case you feel the need to diagnose me, forget about it. There is a long line of people ahead of you.

Whether you or anyone else care to agree about the subject matter covered, and my views about improper behavior, at least I am being honest. That is what I am hoping for when it comes to people who may see themselves or others reflected in any of the topics I have chosen; honest reflection. I am looking for that special someone who is willing to say: "Oh my God, I do that," or "He is talking about me," or "That is exactly how I feel". If you see yourself identified, that is the first step in your recovery. Recognizing your transgressions and continuing to do them is not at all helpful. The whole idea for writing this book is to point out annoyances and to get people to stop doing them, or at least to talk about them. Laughing about them is okay; doing nothing is not. If any of these passages sound familiar enough to you as examples of your own personal conduct, perhaps there is something you should seriously consider – If the shoe fits, wear it! Then stop wearing it, throw it away, and don't wear it anymore.

ATTITUDE

CHAPTER 1
YOUR UNWANTED OPINION

There is an old saying that goes like this: "if I wanted your opinion I would ask for it". I am sure you have probably never heard of it. If you did, you would appreciate what it means to give someone an opinion that they are not interested in receiving. Although I find it hard to believe that this well-known saying is unknown to you, it is a message you should allow to sink in. Perhaps slowly at first, so as not to overwhelm. But please do allow it to become immersed within your soul so that, at the end of the day, one thing is perfectly clear; you really need to keep your opinions to yourself.

For some reason, you seem to think that your view on almost all matters is pure gold. From your mouth comes pearls of wisdom. I am not saying that you don't ever have some good ideas or practical advice. I am not saying that in the least. What I am saying is that you seem to have an opinion about everything and feel that the world will be a much better and happier place if we pay attention to your thoughts and views. As you deliver your golden pearls you are expecting the complete and undivided attention of the intended recipient so that the word of God can be well-considered and completely understood. That is obviously the case given the frequency with which you deliver your orations and the seriousness with which you expect that everyone considers the value of your superior thought and wisdom.

To give an opinion when it is solicited is a good thing. You are doing exactly that which is being requested. In fact, it is an honor to be asked. It means that your opinion is valued. It is treasured. If that isn't an ego-booster, I don't know what is.

1

When you offer an opinion when it is not being requested, you are taking a very big chance that you will offend. When you give an opinion all the time, you are no longer taking a chance. You are guaranteeing you have stepped over the line. You have exceeded the boundaries of that line by a country mile. You are also quite clearly offending, even if nobody is telling you that is the case.

The truth of the matter is that people like to get along and generally don't like to make waves. They are more likely than not to let things pass; even things that they find to be untasteful or problematic. They tolerate difficult subjects for the sake of a friendship or because of a family dynamic that demands that great leeway be extended. And I am not saying that you are stupid and don't have some good ideas every once in a while. What I am saying is that you have an opinion about everything and, for the most part, I want you to keep your opinions to yourself.

You probably think that you do nothing wrong and that you are both courteous and thoughtful in the way in which you extend your thoughtfulness to others. Wrong. Consider this: Do you start the conversation off with a "if you ask me, I would …"? Perhaps you do that or some variation thereof. How thoughtful. How considerate. Bullshit! You don't give me the chance to tell you that I am not asking you. You are so full of yourself and your brilliance that you could not possibly imagine that I have no interest in hearing what you have to say.

Let's turn this around for a second. How would you feel if I gave you my opinion on everything you do and say? How would my thoughts on your life be received by you? Is it possible that you do not value my opinion and that you also believe that your way is the best way to handle every situation that can and will ever come along?

Before you get too defensive, remember this; life works best when it is fair for all concerned parties. What is fair for you may not be fair for me, and vice versa. If I ask for your opinion, it means that I value it and want it. If I don't ask for it, it means I am not looking for it. I look for things I cannot find. I look for things that are lost. Sometimes I would really appreciate it if you could lose your opinion.

CHAPTER 2
ALWAYS A DISAPPOINTMENT

If I ask you to get something, you typically get the wrong thing or the wrong size thing. If you say you are going to do something, you don't do it, you do it wrong, or you come up with some reason why you can't do it at all. When I bring this all to your attention, I get this confused and dazed look. Clearly, something alien has now come before you when I am addressing you on this topic. I get the impression that you aren't trying to side-step the issue. You appear to be genuinely stumped and mystified by how in the world you can be accused of not being a stellar human being or not having accomplished what, to you, is clearly a home run. For you, all that you do is always a job well done. For me and others, we are clearly thinking something else.

Time and again you disappoint me and others by missing appointments, being late, or not doing what you are asked to do. If you suffer a stroke or a heart attack or if you say you can't accomplish a particular task, that is one thing. But when you accept the responsibility of doing something or getting something done and still don't come through, that is something else entirely. You either don't do what you commit to, you don't do it on time, you do it half-assed, or you don't do it at all. The excuses are not wanted. The results surely are.

That being said, I still care very much about you. I do so notwithstanding the fact that you bring about so much disappointment. I might even have come to accept the fact that you are so clueless and hopeless. You can only be disappointed in those persons from whom you have an expectancy. I expect nothing from strangers. I expect nothing from people who really do not know me. From you I expect so much more. I probably shouldn't, but I do.

3

Either at home, in life, or on the job, I expect to receive the same courtesies and results that you would expect to receive from me. If I tell you I will finish something today, that doesn't mean I will finish it tomorrow or three days from now. If you ask me to do something, I will do it efficiently and on time. I actually and frequently go out of my way not to disappoint you. I consider your feelings greatly. Unfortunately, you consider my feelings with the same importance as deciding whether to put butter spray on your popcorn.

Perhaps I am being too harsh in my rant about your behavior. Maybe the problem is not you; it is me and everyone else. Perhaps I have set the bar too high for you. That is my fault, not yours. The only way that setting the bar high for you makes any sense, is if we were dancing the limbo. The higher the bar, the better off you and everyone else will be.

CHAPTER 3
PASSIVE /AGGRESSIVE PEOPLE

I want you to know that it is okay for you to speak your mind. I think our relationship has evolved to the point where we should be receptive to being honest with each other. It is okay and, in fact, desirable to temper the delivery of criticism in order to take the sting out of it. It is best not to criticize all the time because then you sound overly judgmental. Everything done the right way can, hopefully, have the desired effect without any hint of animosity from the person who has had the courage to say something that is often difficult to say.

But the person I describe is not you. You are what is commonly and typically known as a "passive-aggressive". You seem to think that you are sugar coating things when that is definitely not the case. Your message delivery system is more of a combination of a gentle caress and a slap to the face. Sometimes the slap is more of a punch. Sometimes you use certain phrases that let me know it is coming. You say things like: Please don't get me wrong, but…" Or, and we have all heard this one: "No offense, but…' Guess what? Offense taken! Offense taken big time.

There is one other thing that you do that is just plain scary. We can be having a normal conversation and, then, for some reason, you go nutso. You raise your voice and you become irrational in your comments and responses. You simply lose it for no apparent reason. It is as if I have hit a nerve that I didn't know existed and then, bingo, the world has now come to an end. But only briefly, I might add. I am often left wondering; how do I get off this merry-go-round.

5

So, I just wanted to let you know about this thing that you do that freaks me out. You probably think that it is no big deal. It is. You probably think it is better than exploding in one fell swoop. It isn't. Both are bad. Both leave hurt feelings and resentment. Both situations cause rifts that are in need of repair. My preference is that you never allow our relationship to devolve to the point that you can't tell me how you feel about anything. Don't worry, I can take it. What I can't take is passive-aggressiveness. And to show you that I mean what I say, the next time you do it, I am going to kiss you and punch you in the face at the same time.

CHAPTER 4

HAVING A BAD ATTITUDE

Everybody has some sort of an attitude. Some are good, and some are not as good as others. Some are so positive it is beyond belief. There are wildly positive and passionate people who are born leaders. Everyone loves them, and everyone wants to be like them.

And then there are those people who have attitudes that are not so good. They are a bit of a downer. They are generally not the bell of the ball and not the life of the party. You might want to avoid them when you are feeling a bit down. When I think of these negative-nellies, I think of you. You are one of those people. Your attitude is way beyond not so good. To be honest, you have a bad attitude. Wait, I am being polite. What I really mean to say is that you have a bad f#@*&ng attitude. There, I have said it. Quite frankly, I have been meaning to say this to you for a loonnnnngggggg time.

Why haven't I said anything about this before? Well, that just isn't me. I am not the kind of person who likes controversy or confrontation. I would rather sulk or put my tail between my legs and walk away after one of your negative outbursts than tell you what is really on my mind. I would prefer to get along. I am quite confident that, if I did say something it would only make matters worse. I have thought our relationship was one to cherish and I have always been afraid to do anything that might rock the boat.

But you are the one with the problem, not me. You are the one who finds something negative to say about virtually anything and everything; anyone and everyone. You are the person who makes cutting and sarcastic comments at the drop of a hat. You are the one who finds fault for the smallest and most minor things. You are also easily offended

7

and quick to anger; so much so that it somewhat limits our conversations. In fact, I have often thought of getting you one of those small trampolines, so you can get some really good height before you jump down my throat.

If I were to tell you that I don't particularly like something you have done or said, it means I am being honest with you and letting you know my thoughts on the subject. It doesn't mean I have a bad attitude. Honesty doesn't mean you have a bad attitude. It means you are being truthful; big difference! Is that okay that I am being honest? Isn't that the way it should be? Or are you expecting that everything you say to be considered solid gold and everything I say to be irrelevant? If I don't like something and I express it to you, it doesn't mean I don't like you or that I always think that your thought process for just about everything is fatally flawed. Get It?! But that is not the point. I am always walking on eggshells, hoping and praying that you will not find fault with what I hope to be a constructive reaction and thoughtful conversation. Usually and unfortunately, I am wrong for thinking and hoping for the best. Is that any way to have a meaningful relationship?

I am asking you very nicely to please consider your actions and my feelings for a change. You probably think that you already do that. You would like to think that you are not a negative person. Surprise! You are about as negative as an integer can get. Being around you is as desirable as a double root canal. There was that one time you actually were 100% positive throughout our conversation. It was both surprising and refreshing. However, for the most part, that is rarely the case.

If you are insulted by this revelation to you, and it affects our relationship in a bad way, then I guess we really didn't have anything all that special to begin with. Hopefully you will take some action to put me at ease and take our relationship to a whole new and better level. I am hoping for the best. If your response to reading this is that I am the one with a bad attitude, I suppose you are right. But you are the one who gave it to me!

CHAPTER 5

YOU SUCK

You suck. There really is no reason to sugarcoat it and there really is nothing more to say.

CHAPTER 6

LIAR, LIAR PANTS ON FIRE

In case you are thinking of telling me something now or anytime in the future, I want you to know that, no matter what it is, I do not believe it to be true. It does not matter what it is. It could be something as mundane as you couldn't find your coat this morning or you snapped your dental floss while flossing. It really doesn't matter. It pains me to say it, but I cannot believe a single word that you say.

It all boils down to the fact that you are, without a doubt, the biggest liar known to mankind. You are pathological. With you it is a disease. I don't take what you say with a grain of salt. I take it to the bathroom and flush it down the toilet. That is what it is worth.

To you there is no such thing as "the truth". You have no idea what it means. You wouldn't know it if it hit you upside your head and turned around and hit you on the side of the head it missed. You appear to have accepted your disability by the adoption of an alternative approach to reality. To you it is not a mere exaggeration or even a white lie. It is not even or remotely a falsehood. It is a semi-inaccurate portrayal and partial mislabeling of a factual depiction of what might otherwise be understood to be reality. But that is how you might see or perceive it. And we all know that perception is subjective. So, anything you do is subject to other people's perception of your reality and your warped view and understanding of life. The fact that they inaccurately see things is their problem, not yours.

I am sure you see some credence and rationale to your ridiculous way of meandering through life. It is total nonsense to the rest of us. You are a fraud, pure and simple.

And the worst part is, you are oblivious to your falsehoods to the point that you don't even bat an eye if someone catches you in the act. To you, it is no big deal. Why did you say you drove here when I saw you get off a bus? To you the question is irrelevant. What does that have to do with whether you are having chicken or steak for dinner. It is nonsensical to you. You have altered your internal brain to make it so that the stars align with your version of planet false-itis. What seems patently untrue and ridiculous to everyone else is easily explainable by you in your warped sense of reality.

And for you the best part is when people become accustomed to your lying. So much so that they have given up calling you out on it each and every time it occurs. That must really be a great feeling on your part. It must be so awesome to know that you can live in a make-believe world and everyone is playing along with you. Well, guess what? I'm not and neither is anyone else. We all think you are a fraud. You are a lying SOB, and everyone knows it. You are tolerated mostly because we are not mean enough to give you the old heave-ho. But that is exactly what we would be doing if we were to be honest and (here is something you won't understand) truthful with you. We have sucked it up long enough and it is high time that you got a taste of your own medicine. Get ready for massive spoonful's because there isn't enough sugar to help that kind of medicine go down when you are a perpetually lying sack of shit.

CHAPTER 7
ACKNOWLEDGING WHEN YOU MAKE MISTAKES AND ARE WRONG

I have made a lot of dumb mistakes. The list is very, very long. I also know that I am not the only person in the world who is the victim of his own stupidity. Have you ever driven 2 hours to a ballgame and left the tickets at home? Have you ever gone grocery shopping and returned with everything but the one thing that was your main purpose for visiting the store in the first place? Have you ever said something mean, off-color or totally inappropriate and, as the words slowly leaked out, you seriously considered stuffing them back in your mouth?

Some of my faux pas were absolutely humongous and, thankfully, known only to me because I covered my tracks so beautifully. Some, to the trained eye, were not mistakes at all. Maybe they are best characterized as little boo boos or minor mental lapses. When I do make mistakes, I frequently tell myself that I am stupid, an idiot, a dummy or something significantly worse. Sometimes I really let myself have it. I beat myself up for hours on end and often for days. The name-calling is not reserved for only me, as I have been the beneficiary of similar insults from many others during the course of my life. Some of the barbs made sense at the time. Others did not. One of my favorites came from a former boss who told me that what I said, "was the stupidest thing (he had) ever heard." I replied, without hesitation, that, "if (he waited) a minute, I (was) certain that I could top it."

I am acknowledging my innermost and far too frequent transgressions for a very good reason. I make mistakes. I make a ton of them. I acknowledge them to myself and to others. But what about you?

I do not get the sense that you take any responsibility for your wrongful actions. None whatsoever. Perhaps you acknowledge it to yourself; however, even if that were the case, it would appear that nothing you ever do is your fault or any big deal. You have never said you were wrong. Is this because of some linguistic disassociation you have with vocalizing certain words that begin with the letter "W" (for wrong) or "S" (for sorry)?? Were you traumatized as a child when you did something bad and swore you would never own up to anything again? Were whips and chains involved?

The truth of the matter is that when you do admit your failings, a veil is lifted, and you can move on. Otherwise the tension persists. People come to expect that you will never admit the truth. The problem with that is that they don't know if you recognize the error of your ways. If you don't see yourself as having made a mistake, then you are likely to do it again. History will repeat itself and it will all happen because you are either oblivious to reality or a stubborn fool. Which one are you?

I understand that when people point out your shortcomings it is totally unappreciated. I totally get that. Get over it and move on. That is what I do and so does everyone else in the universe. When you can't seem to acknowledge your misdeeds everyone wonders why that is the case. They think something is wrong with you. You can't be trusted to do what is right when you do not seem to appreciate when something is wrong. If you secretly know it is and aren't letting on, that is a one-sided conversation that is having zero benefit.

Just for giggles, see what it is like to admit to your failings and see how you feel and how people react to you when you do. Initially you may be met with disbelief from those who have never seen that side of you. But, eventually, they will come to see a new you and let you into that part of their world where you were otherwise forbidden to enter. The welcome mat will be extended. Your life might actually become more fulfilling. Either that or you can just continue disavowing all your transgressions. For the most part, I know in which direction you will head. After all, how could you possibly admit to being wrong when, according to you, you never really are?

CHAPTER 8

FAIRWEATHER FRIENDS

Did you hear I was in the hospital? Did you know that there was a death in my family? If you were aware of either of these circumstances, I thought you should also be aware that I am now doing okay, although things were pretty tough there for a while. I am now, thankfully, in a better position to be able to reflect on things. While reflecting, something important just dawned on me; you never bothered to reach out to me even once while I was dealing with my nightmare. Whether you knew or didn't know what was going on, where the hell have you been?

You are what is known as a "Fairweather Friend". You come in and out of people's lives as it suits you. If things get a little too heavy, you drop out for a bit so as not to be too overwhelmed with other people's stuff. You have your own baggage and God forbid you add someone else's issues to your own. Your motto is a good one (for you) – when the going gets tough, you get going.

I have stopped wondering where you are or what you are doing because my thoughts and concerns for you have waned over the years in direct proportion to the diminishing love that is sent my way. I include you in my circle of friends, but there are times that you might be considered more of an "acquaintance". It isn't that I prefer it that way, it is simply more attributable to the fact that what we treasure is more like a season of baseball than a trusted and valued friendship. Only when things start heating up and getting exciting do you seem to be well-connected with me. Otherwise, you make little to no effort to see if I am alive.

Maybe our friendship is just a tribute to the past and we are allowing our former glory to keep a flicker of a flame alive. Maybe we should just let it die. That is not my preference, but it certainly seems to be yours. I know that people change, and you can't relive the past. But you can and should be able to count on those people who are important in your life who are willing to give you the shirt off their back. There is a difference between people who are friends or acquaintances, and those special people you can count on one hand who you know to be trusted and the dearest of friends. The ones who check in on you frequently and get together with you from time to time. The ones who make an effort and show you that they care. The special people who are there for you when you really need someone and are at your absolute worst. Those are the people you want and need in your life. All others are superfluous, unnecessary, and, like you, "Fairweather Friends".

As I get older, I realize how precious time is and how important it is to not waste it on those who don't deserve it. I am going to spend my time with "All-weather Friends," who will be with me through thick and thin. Asking someone to extend themselves to give more than what they are already doing may seem like a great inconvenience. To a part-time employee, that may be the case; but not to a good friend. It doesn't require money or the owning of a car to have a great friendship. It requires an effort; a continuous, ongoing and meaningful one.

If you want to be a friend to people, be a good one. Be a person that shows that you care. If you want to do as you please and to jump in and out of people's lives as you deem fit, don't be surprised if one day you find the door closed and you aren't allowed in anymore. By then it may be too late to undo the harm that your care-free attitude has caused. The choice is yours. Be there through all kinds of weather, not just when the skies are sunny and bright.

CLEANLINESS

CHAPTER 9

NOT WASHING YOUR HANDS AFTER YOU GO TO THE BATHROOM

I know you don't think this is any big deal, but I can't stand the fact that you don't wash your hands after you go to the bathroom. I have even mentioned it to you and you have poo-pooed (Ha! Ha!) what I have to say about this subject.

I have a feeling that you think there is a distinction between going # 1 or going #2. If you go #1 and don't pee on your hands, then I guess you think that you don't need to wash them. But, for some reason, you also seem to think that when you go # 2 you do need to wash after you are done (at least I hope you do). I don't get it, what is the difference between not crapping and not peeing on your hands? Why would you wash after one and not the other? Unless, of course, you don't wash after either going #1 or #2. At least be consistent.

And let me ask you this; did you touch the handle in order to complete the process? Who touched the handle before you and what was the nature of the business they concluded before they did their handle touching? Is it possible that they are a germ carrying deviant or some kind of germ-free angel the likes of which we have never seen before?

What you have also failed to consider is that whatever you do in your home is exactly what you will do when you go in the privacy of another person's home or in a public facility. When you touch the handle after you are done, you are touching the germs from someone else. When you open and close the bathroom door, you are touching the germs belonging to many other people. When you open and close a bathroom stall, you are communing with germ city as well. And that doesn't gross you out?

The bottom line is this; you have some seriously bad bathroom-going etiquette. You are spreading your germs and the germs of others all over the place. This needs to stop. And here is something else you may not know; everyone in your family and at your workplace knows that you are a non-washer. They talk about you and they keep their distance from you. If that gives you pause, then do something about your poor toilet habits. If you still don't care, remember this, I will fist-bump you, but don't ever ask me to shake your hand.

CHAPTER 10
MESSY BATHROOM SINK

Look around you and you will see that there is tremendous beauty in this world. Almost anywhere you look you will see things that can be truly awe-inspiring. There are also places you can go where you will see things that are most unpleasant. They may even cause you to recoil in horror. Your bathroom sink would be one of those places.

Your sink is a special place the likes of which nobody should ever see. It has amassed an array of things that are layered over what once was a pristine and well-polished thing of beauty.

There is dried up toothpaste all over the place. The good news is that you use toothpaste. The bad news is that you will probably need a chisel to remove it. Besides toothpaste there is also all kinds of caked on soap, dirt, makeup, hair and other things I do not recognize as being of this earth. Your sink is truly disgusting. One might be better off washing in your toilet than using this gross looking basin. Now that I think of it, your bathroom floor is nothing special either.

I realize it is your sink and you can do whatever you want with it. It is personal to you and what you do with your stuff is your business. I get that. I see great truth in that concept. But there is another truth that underlies your disgusting behavior. That is the truth that you do not care about such things. If you don't care about how messy you are, what else do you not care about?

Maybe you think this is all much ado about nothing. Why would anyone care about what you do in the privacy of your own home? I suppose that is true. Generally, these are the types of things that people laugh about at bars and at comedy shows. But this is no laughing matter. For some reason, you think nothing of leaving your place untidy and messy and allowing me (and lord knows who else) to see what you consider to be status quo. It doesn't say very much about you and it says even less about how you feel about me. You have some disgusting personal habits and I not only know about them, you want me to know about them. It doesn't matter how nice you look to the outside world; your true inner self is sitting like a grease pit in your bathroom sink and elsewhere.

This is an opportunity for you to do a little inner retrospection. Your bathroom sink is a reflection of the real you. Do you like it? Do you care? I feel like I have done all that I can in pointing out to you what I am seeing, and it is up to you to do, or not do, something about it. As for me, I also have a choice; I am never going into your bathroom again.

CHAPTER 11

EATING IN BED

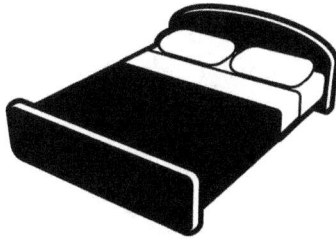

Did you ever get under the sheets and feel something crunchy, gooey or icky between your toes or against your hands or fingers? At first you are startled. After all, it isn't what you expect to find in bed. You expect to feel nice, crisp and clean nothingness from one end of the bed to the other. You certainly do not expect to find part of a pop tart, the filling from an Oreo, a gum wrapper, an apple core, popcorn kernels, Doritos, M & M's, a piece of licorice, a gummy bear, and lord knows what else. You go from startled to freaked out in a Nano-second. You will be unable to rest without resolving the problem or going elsewhere for a more peaceful sleep. You know there is food in the bed; you also know it didn't get there of its own accord. Someone put it there and you know that someone was not you.

There are probably some people who find this all to be ridiculous, a sign of extreme over-reaction and, perhaps, melodramatic. They see nothing wrong with this. These are the same people who go to the beach and bring their sandy feet into bed without washing them (we will leave that for another day). They leave their stuff all over the floor, leave dishes in the sink, dust every blue moon, and generally cannot understand for the life of them why people make such a fuss over such things.

On the scale of things, I can appreciate the fact that the world has a great many other more important problems that demand our attention. The fact that someone likes to snack in bed is, in the scheme of things, a fleck on the wing of a gnat.

To those who eat in bed, this may all be true. To most everyone else in the universe, they prefer to dine in the parts of a home that are designated for such purposes. You don't put your bed in the dining room, unless, of course, your place is so small that there is no dining room. But regardless of the size of your home, people generally set aside a spot for consuming food. They then retire to the bathroom, brush their teeth, then go to bed. Those who eat in bed are either eating after brushing, not brushing, or never-ending eaters.

Regardless of where you stand on the dental and health management side of life, if you eat in bed you are doing the same thing as certain animals. They crap where they eat. It isn't exactly the same, but it is definitely crap. Think about that the next time you decide you need to munch on some peanuts and left-over fries just before you say your lullabies.

CHAPTER 12

LEAVING YOUR STUFF
ALL OVER THE PLACE

The other day I went to one of those big box stores to buy a few things that I needed. As I was walking around I came across their furniture section. I was amazed by all the dressers, credenzas, bookcases and closet organizing gadgetry that they had for purchase. Some of these items were quite pricey. Others were more affordable and ingenious. While exploring additional aisles at the store, I got to thinking about what I would do with all these drawers and organizers. I could see many useful purposes. And then I started thinking about what you would do with them. Believe it or not, I was stumped. I really did not think they would benefit you in the least.

The reason why I think this way is because of the manner in which you live your life. Your clothing, papers, books and just about everything else you own are all on the floor and all over the place. Yes, you do have some things that are in drawers or hanging in closets. But I am not sure why that is the case. They are either in these locations because you do not need or want them or because they are soon destined to lie on the floor. You are just waiting for the right moment to excommunicate them from their current location.

I really do not understand why you think people have bedrooms and office furniture. You do not use them effectively. They must be nothing more than a nuisance to you. If you have stuff on a shelf, in a drawer or in a closet, perhaps you consider them dead. It is as if they do not exist. The only things that matter to you are the things you can see. Granted some of the things you might want to see are buried under other things; but that is beside the point. By not hiding in a drawer or a closet, the things that are open to your view have the best chance of seeing the light of your day. You are actually doing your possessions a favor by exposing them to the world as much as you possibly can by not placing them in a storage device. Visibility enhances usefulness; I get it.

I suppose you are unimpressed by the fact that stuff on the ground makes it difficult to navigate around the place. There is a significant likelihood that your stuff might actually get stepped on and become soiled during the process. I really do not think that you care about that. Clothing can always be washed, folded (or not folded) and then thrown back on the floor. You may be able to clean things that get dirty, but who cares, anyway?!

I have always wondered whether you liked to have stuff on the floor moved so the floor beneath it can be cleaned. That would be the equivalent of organizing the disorganization of disorderly stuff. If it is moved, then it will just lie somewhere else. You can't seriously be concerned about where on the floor things will lie. Whether it is here or there, what difference does it make? I would think that adding an element of organization to the situation would be okay as long as your worldly possessions were visible, and you knew it was not in a drawer or a closet.

You would be best served if there was more available space to throw things every which way. Since your bookshelves and dressers are meaningless in the scheme of things, perhaps you should consider getting rid of them. Whatever is in them you can throw on the floor to join their other family members. You could use the extra space for the Woodstock crap festival on the floor. Besides, more things on the floor will create a nice reunion for stuff in the drawers and shelves that have not seen their counterparts for a long, long time. These long-forgotten things will have conversations with their long-lost cousins and friends. Surely, they would all want to know that they are okay and doing fine. Your stuff would then be as happy as you are. Happy and messy. Just the way you like it.

CHAPTER 13

HAIR IN THE TUB OR SHOWER

The other day I went into the bathroom to take a shower. I turned on the water and brushed my teeth while waiting for the water to get hot. I stepped into the shower only to find that I was wading in 3 inches of water. Apparently, the shower was not properly draining. That is because the drain was clogged with hair.

I cannot understand how you can possibly take a shower and accumulate so much hair. If the shower fills up with water before I get in, then it must have been that way when you last got out. I know you think it is my hair and not yours. That is why you won't touch it. In case you didn't know, you could use a paper towel or some toilet paper to assist. I can show you where you can find such things in case you become disoriented and can't find them.

I suppose there is also a possibility that you know it is your hair, but you just can't be bothered performing an unclogging. It is really a big project, if you think about it. First you need to recognize there is hair in the drain. Then you need to use your hands, feet or some other object to remove the hair from the drain. This might require a sweeping foot movement or a bending of the torso. Exertion will be required in some form. A nap will be required thereafter.

If you do not heed my request, you will force me to wait you out with a little game we will now call "what hair in the shower?" In this game, we will both pretend we do not notice any hair clogging the drain. We will both take showers in a pool of standing, dirty water. There will be so much hair built up in the drain area that the shower will never drain.

Eventually, we will both be so grossed out by our shower that we will no longer take showers. We will become "stinky" annoyances to each other and everyone else. Eventually, one of us will crack or we will just have to move away. Is that what you want? If yes, game on! If not, you know what to do.

CHAPTER 14

SPITTING ON THE GROUND

Baseball players are obviously the ones that most immediately come to mind when anyone thinks about people who seem to love to spit on the ground. There are players who chew tobacco and spit and those who spit just for the hell of it. They seem fairly expert at the craft, but not good enough that they can do it on the run like a horse can drop a load. I think that has something to do with wind direction and back spray. Maybe those who are truly pros can do this, but I haven't studied the art of spittle to that extent.

I can assure you that, when at home or out to a restaurant with friends or family, these same ballplayers are not conducting themselves in the same manner as we typically see them at the park. They don't lean over to the side of the table at a fine dining establishment and chuck a loogie between theirs and the next table. They don't sit quietly at home in their den or study and spit on the carpet, hardwood or tile either. At home and when out with others, they act like a respectable person might be expected to conduct themselves. They are refined and distinguished. They are exactly the opposite of what you see during the game. Hard to believe, but true.

What I want to know is how is it possible that people like you and ballplayers can act so disgustingly in one venue and so posh in another? Surely when you are outside of your dirt or street venue, you must go into withdrawal. That has to be the case. If it is an obsession or compulsion in one place, how can you possibly turn it off when you are in another? If you can't spit out the window when you are driving, what do you do?

29

Surely when you are out to dinner with an important person you must be thinking that if the evening lasts one more minute you are going to spew a river. How can you speak with all that is building up inside your loogie-filled orifice? You must be dreaming of leaving the venue as quickly as possible, so you can relieve your throaty hose while spitting your way fantastic all the merry way home.

Seriously, what is going on inside that head of yours? How does this make sense? How do you not see that this is nasty, disgusting and incredibly gross? How can you not appreciate that everyone who sees you doing this is thinking something other than, whoa, what a charming and well-polished human being? They are also possibly wondering if you want some clam sauce to go along with the rest of that meal.

I don't know if you ever thought about it, but wherever you spit someone may step or even unintentionally fall. They will, unwittingly, come in contact with your DNA. They will become a part of something that isn't just a bad habit. It is a totally controllable bodily discharge that you can obviously turn on and off like a faucet. If you closed your eyes and didn't know where you were, I guarantee you that you wouldn't dig deep for a nice throaty propulsion until you could be sure that it had a proper landing place. So, it isn't about need; it is about place. It is totally controllable. You simply choose to do it or not do it.

Aside from the fact that you look ridiculous and are an embarrassment to yourself and all others with whom you are associated, maybe you should consider stopping this nonsensical and severely disgusting bad-habit. Instead of spitting things out of your mouth, why not use it for its intended purpose; eating and speaking. Instead of a wet discharge, try using your orifice for a good meal and witty conversation. You, the ground and the world will be a whole lot better off.

CHAPTER 15

CLOSING DRAWERS AND DOORS

I know I sound like a broken record, but I would greatly appreciate it if you would please close the drawers and doors that you open. I realize you don't think it is any big deal, but it drives me crazy. There are actually some practical considerations for heeding my request. My reasoning is as follows:

1. When you leave drawers and doors open, they are not closed. I like them closed.

2. When they are open, they look unkempt and untidy. They suggest a lack of order. As you know, I am into orderliness in a big way. They even have a television show by that name – "Law and Order". In my mind, the law of this place is that we must have order. Please obey the law.

3. Open drawers and doors show a complete disregard for the proper way to maintain a home or place of business. Anyone who thinks drawers and doors can be left open would also have no issue with a dusty house, throwing clothes on the floor or leaving things messy. If you want to make sure everyone knows the kind of person you really are, keep drawers and doors wide open.

4. People can bump their heads on open cabinet doors and they can hurt themselves when bumping into open drawers. The reasons why these bumps and bruises occur are because normal people do not expect these things to be open. Do you understand? Closed IS normal; open is NOT normal!!! Closed is good; open is bad. If you keep things open, you will make me mad!

5. An open drawer is an opportunity for even greater messiness. If you leave a drawer open in the kitchen and slice a loaf of bread nearby, the crumbs are likely to find their way into the drawer. That means you have made things more difficult for yourself. You will need to clean crumbs on the counter, the floor and the drawer. The only way to really clean the drawer is to take everything out of it. Unless, of course, you like things messy. In that case, crumbs in the drawer are really no biggie.

6. I have left the most important reason for last. An open door and drawer is a direct portal for every monster in the universe. It is also a quick entranceway for the boogie man.

Like they say in Law and Order – "case closed".

DRIVING

CHAPTER 16

PARKING YOUR CAR

I don't know if you realize it, but the zoning laws of virtually every city and town in the United States prescribe the width and length for all parking spaces. These rules actually have some historical basis and typify the approximate area one would need to safely park, exit and enter a car in a parked space.

Why am I telling you this? Because you seem to think that the parking rules that apply for all cities and towns are out of touch with reality. I know this because it does not matter how wide a parking space may be; you cannot seem to park your car within that space without overextending your vehicle within the lines of an adjoining space or allowing for a suitable distance between your vehicle and another in the next space.

If the reason why you do this has something to do with the fact that your car is your baby and you don't want anyone to touch it or come near to it, here are a few things for you to consider: try parking a mile away in no-man's land; get a cheaper car; or take the bus. If you are in a rush and need to just get in and out quickly, nobody gives a crap. They do care if you park like a moron. When you overextend a space, you are impacting everyone else. It is like a domino effect. Everyone needs to compensate for your stupidity. Everyone is thinking your car is parked by a 4-year old that has a real jerk as an owner.

Lastly, it may very well be the case that you have some serious spatial relations issues and you simply do not have the wherewithal to effectively navigate spaces. If that is the case, get a smaller car or a motorcycle. Please be aware that driving a car is a privilege. Some people do not qualify for the right to have such a privilege. You might actually be one of them.

CHAPTER 17

STAY OUT OF THE PASSING LANE

Every time I see traffic on any multiple lane road or highway, I always think that there is some bozo at the head of the passing lane who is going way too slow. You can see there is a clear path in front of them for a thousand feet. But they just keep on their merry way, oblivious to the anger they are creating behind them. In case you didn't know it, that bozo is you.

By definition, the passing lane is the one closest to the center line (or median) of a highway. It is called a 'passing lane' because it is to be used (get this) for passing. It is not to be used as a 'traveling lane'.

Some people think that the passing lane is the 'high-speed lane'. They are incorrect in their understanding. But that doesn't really matter, because you obviously are not in the high-speed camp. You seem to feel that the road is yours to do as you please. If you want to go slowly in the lane of your choice, that is your prerogative. If you are going the speed limit in the passing lane and someone wants to pass you, tough luck. They will have to either go around you or suffer their journey at your pace and speed. In fact, you think you are doing them a favor by helping them to not break the law. You seem to be of the opinion that, if you wouldn't buy alcohol for a minor, why should you help strangers exceed the speed limit. You think you are a good Samaritan. Truth be told; you are a pain the ass.

By driving the speed you deem to be appropriate in the passing lane, you are contributing to a number of negative consequences.

They might include the following: someone being late for work; making it difficult for someone to timely get to the next exit for a restroom break; and impeding the progress of someone who desperately needs to get to a hospital. Because of your selfishness, someone may lose their job, crap their pants, or deliver a baby in the backseat of their car. How does that make you feel?

Perhaps you might want to consider the ramifications of your actions the next time you travel in the passing lane and see the flashing lights of the car behind you that is desperately trying to get your attention and begging you to pull over. Perhaps you also might want to pay attention to the beeping horn of the same car that is about to lose it with you because you have ignored their flashing lights. If you should decide to honor their request and move over, please do so in quickly. Do not put on your blinker for a week and a half and make believe you are seeking the right moment for a smooth transition to another lane. We are impatiently seething about the 10 to 15 opportunities you have allowed to pass you by in your make-believe attempt to do what you should have been doing all along.

If someone wants to get by you, please be a good Samaritan and help them out. Although you might think otherwise, you were not put on this earth to judge us or to prevent people from exceeding the speed limit. If they want to run the risk of getting a ticket for doing so, that is their business. It is most definitely not yours. You belong in the other lane along with all the other slow drivers. Why? Because you are a feather-foot, and birds of a feather should stick together.

CHAPTER 18

USING YOUR TURN SIGNALS

I don't know about you, but when I am driving and looking to take a left or a right, or if I am looking to move over to a lane, I flip on my turn signal well in advance of doing so. I do this for a couple of reasons: it is a matter of common courtesy and, believe it or not, it is the law. The former reason is not something that should mean a whole lot to you given your general lack of disregard for typical social decorum. The second reason probably doesn't mean very much to you either, but definitely will when you find yourself on the side of the road talking to someone with a badge and a gun who is asking to see your driver's license and registration.

For you, the use of a turn signal, is a nuisance. You use it sporadically and only if you feel like it. For the most part, the spirit rarely moves you in that direction – the direction of the turn signal. Just so you know, this is an often-used electronic device that allows the person to the left, right and behind you to know of your intentions. You could always teleport yourself into their car and tell them, or call them on the phone if you have their number; however, since neither of those scenarios is likely to be the case, the electronic turn signal serves as your secret coded notification that you are about to do something.

Assuming that you actually studied for and received a valid driver's license, there are arm signals you learned to use for turns. There is even an arm signal if you want to come to a complete stop and you have no brake lights. Do you remember any of that? These are perfectly fine and acceptable alternatives to your use of blinkers. They are especially helpful if your turn signal is broken. If your arm is broken, you can use your turn signal and you can use your turn signal even if your arm isn't broken. Your options are actually quite extensive. It is even fun to use arm signals during snow storms and hurricanes. Nobody expects it and they probably can hardly see you anyway.

Using your turn signal is not only about the law and a matter of common courtesy. If I decide to move up on your left and you are planning to come into my lane without proper notification, an accident can potentially occur. And do you know who will be at fault? YOU!!!!!!!!!!!!!!!!! But you won't see it that way. People like you never do. You always think it is someone else's fault. In your mind, the following things have happened: they should have seen you moving over; they were speeding; you were in a blind spot; and they came upon you suddenly and you didn't have a reasonable time to react. You will have an untold number of excuses; all of them wrong.

Believe it or not, use of the turn signal is a well-known commodity that is both recognized and appreciated by one and all. Please do yourself and everyone else a favor; obey the law and do what everyone else around you is doing when they decide to move from one lane to another. Take advantage of the opportunity to use that incredibly special communication device that you have been provided to engage with others in the course of your travels. Because of the message that a turn signal delivers, courtesies are extended by strangers who will slow up and let you in because they have more than a clue as to your intentions. Once you get into the swing of things, it will also be appreciated ever much more than the middle-finger salute you receive when you choose to change lanes without it.

CHAPTER 19

TAIL-GATING

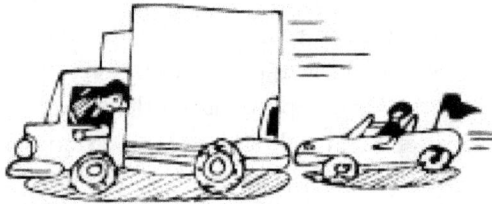

Did you ever take a look out your rear-view mirror and notice that the person who is driving behind you is so close that you can smell their breath? That person in the mirror is you. It is your mug that we all see. You are what is commonly known in the business as an ass-riding tail-gater, and you are hated and despised universally.

There are two things that are going on when you are riding inches behind another car; you are thinking 'what the hell is the matter with them, why don't they move?'; and they are thinking 'what the hell is the matter with you, why don't you back off?'' Both of these thought processes are going on simultaneously. While everyone can appreciate why you feel the way you do—because you are an impatient ass—did it ever occur to you that there may be a good reason why the car in front of you is proceeding no faster than their current rate of speed? Did you consider that, if ever they were inclined to move over, you just gave them a reason not to? Or how about this: they can't move over because it isn't safe to do so.

Maybe you think about these things. Maybe you don't. Maybe you just don't care. Maybe you think it is safe for you to move over because you drive like a lunatic and lunatic safety is on a different level from what others consider to be reasonable and safe driving. Maybe others don't feel the way you do. But who cares about others anyway? All you care about is you. All you know is that the lane you are in is your personal space and anyone who is in it is an alien invader that must be brought into a battle that is probably the furthest thing from their mind. You want to engage them in your war. Some may seek to return your volley and, in so doing, the game is on. Is that why you do it? Do you like the game? Or does the game annoy you? Or does it depend upon where you are going and how quickly you want to get there? Perhaps you have to be in the mood for a battle and, if not in the mood, you will simply change lanes and become Mr. or Ms. Pac-man.

Just so you know, automobiles are not bumper cars. You need to go to the amusement park if you are looking for that kind of action. You need to be a good citizen of the road and show good manners while driving on our nation's highways. Do not tailgate. Back-off! You should be giving the same kind of respect that you expect others to show to you. If you insist upon being an inconsiderate bastard, do not be surprised when the lack of courtesy you extend to others is returned to you in spades. It would be nice, for a change, for someone to ride your ass. See what it is like when someone drives so close you can see their nose hairs in your rear-view mirror.

ETIQUETTE

CHAPTER 20

CHANGING THE TOILET
PAPER ROLL

If it is not too much to ask, I would really appreciate it if you would be so kind as to change the toilet paper roll when it is near the end. I am not talking about when there are no sheets at all; although even that situation seems to present as somewhat of a challenge to you. Sometimes you actually do change the roll when it gets to that point, but I think that is probably out of need vs. kindness to others.

So, what does it mean to be near the end? Do you really have to ask? It means when there are only a few sheets on the roll or even less than that. What do I mean by a few? You have got to be kidding! Put it this way; if you can kind of see the cardboard thingy at the end of the roll, you better be thinking that a new roll might be needed. Do you like doing your business only to find there isn't enough paper to get the job done? Well, guess what? Nobody else likes that either.

I want to be clear that I am not asking for you to overextend yourself. If I could even only get you to put a replacement roll somewhere within a few feet of where it needs to go, that would also be acceptable. It is not all that I hope for, but, in your case, it would be a huge undertaking for which I would be truly grateful.

And while I am at it, if I could possibly get you to replace the roll, perhaps I could also get you to install it in the right way. By this I mean that the roll must unroll from the top. Why? Because I said so. It makes me crazy when it unrolls from the backside of the roll. In fact, the federal government recently completed research (costing millions of taxpayer dollars) which proved that tearing from the top uses less paper than if you tear it from the backside. Besides this overwhelming and conclusive research, whoever allows a replaced roll to unravel in such a fashion is obviously totally unconcerned with proper unfolding toilet paper etiquette. Considering the fact that you hardly replace the roll anyway, your upside-down roll placement does not come as too much of a surprise.

Your toilet paper misdeeds are not the only thing you do that is upsetting and aggravating. It is actually only the tip of the iceberg. Thoughtless people who do not have the decency to "replace the roll" have all kinds of other serious psychological problems that would sufficiently put a therapist's children through college. Consider this a head start on your road to a better life and good mental health. The next time you visit the throne room, make sure you leave it for the next king or queen who finds it necessary to embark on royal business.

CHAPTER 21

SAYING THANK YOU TO PEOPLE WHO LET YOU GO BY

Were you ever in a bit of traffic at an intersection or in an area where there were many cars seeking to enter the flow of traffic from a parking area or an on-ramp? Were you ever in a shopping center and saw someone walking to or from their car across the flow of traffic? Most of us have experienced this situation in our lives and, for many people, it happens to them on a daily basis. We see someone who is looking to get somewhere, either on foot or in their car. They are waiting patiently as everyone passes them by. At an intersection or exiting onto a main roadway they try to inch their way forward into traffic but nobody, it seems, wants to let them in.

And then along comes that good Samaritan who graciously slows down and allows the person seeking to pass or cross to get to their intended place and destination. The person looking to cross, or pass, may see the Samaritan slowing down for them and they proceed with a quick and thankful gesture. Sometimes there is no movement at all for fear that intentions have been misread. In that case, the Samaritan is often required to make some sort of a gesture to let them know all is good – hey buddy; it is okay. You are free to go.

So, what happens next after you allow someone to pass? For the most part, they acknowledge you in some fashion with a wave of their hand or a gracious shaking of their head. Sometimes you might even get a thumbs up. They are duly noting a kindness. They are saying thank you. You may even give them a "your welcome" nod in return.

47

The people who are appreciative of someone letting them go by are, what we like to call "normal folk". You, on the other hand, are not. You never seem to appreciate the kindness of people who are, quite literally, in the driver's seat. They could ignore your situation and make you wait until the cows come home. But when they do help out, you act as though they owe you their lives. Guess what? They don't! They are extending to you a courtesy. Therefore, you should also show some graciousness in return. It isn't like it is a huge and monumental task to give thanks with the wave of your hand or the nod of your head. You should try doing it sometime. Initially it will be painful and awkward for you because of the lack of dexterity in that part of your anatomy. Eventually you will get it and it will no longer be such a challenge.

In lieu of trying to be a little more thankful in life, you could carry on as you typically do with no appreciation for the kindness of others. In that case, you should be prepared for quite a bit of payback. You see, what you fail to understand is that the person who extends to you a courtesy is EXPECTING to receive your thanks. When they don't get it, they make a mental note of you. They will go out of their way the next time to not be nice to you. If that is what you are hoping for, your wish will be their command.

CHAPTER 22

ALWAYS LATE

It probably doesn't bother you very much to know this, but I and everyone else hate the fact that you are always late. It doesn't matter what the event might be, we can count on not counting on you to be on time.

When I say, "on time," what I mean is within close proximity to the hour given for your attendance at an event. If you arrive within 5 minutes of the start time, that is well within acceptable margins. That is not "on time," however, for you it will suffice. Occasionally going slightly outside of the 5-minute rule is even okay. But that doesn't matter because you are never occasionally late. You are ALWAYS late. And I don't mean that you arrive 6 minutes late. With you it could be 15 minutes or even an hour past the time you were asked to bless us with your presence.

We all often wonder why it is that you even bother asking about planned start times. What difference does it make to you? Perhaps you need to know so you can make sure that you don't get there too soon. Is that how this works? I don't know, I am just asking. I am wondering why you think your time is so much more valuable than everyone else's. I am wondering why you take such great pleasure in knowing that we are all waiting around for you to arrive. By the way, in case you didn't know, when we are waiting for you we are also talking about how rude and inconsiderate you are. We also always kick ourselves for not giving you an earlier target time so that you might actually arrive when you are supposed to.

In your defense, there are people in this world who expect everyone to be exactly on time and they go bonkers when you are even 7 seconds late. They hold up their watch and tap it, so you get their message. These are the same people who are always early for everything. I suppose they have their own little issues and they should probably get them checked out by a professional.

But I am not talking about obsessively punctual people. I am talking about obsessively and incredibly late people like you. You have a very bad and annoying habit that deserves immediate attention. Hopefully you will do something about this. We all joke that "you will be late for your own funeral". We may be waiting for someone on that sad, sad day; but, finally and for this one time only, at least it won't be you.

CHAPTER 23

GIVE IT BACK

I don't know how good your memory is, but mine is at least good enough that I remember that there is an unwritten rule as to what a person must do after they ask someone if they can borrow something for a special purpose or occasion. They usually visit or call the person and let them know why the borrowing is required. There may be some discussion about how long it will be needed and even how it might match something else if it is being worn. But there is no doubt, once the mission is complete, that which was taken will most certainly be returned.

Except, of course, in your case. When it comes to you, norms are out the window. Because you have something of mine that you have not returned for far too long, here are the possible reasons why that might be the case:

- When you borrowed it in the first place you never intended to give it back;
- You always planned on giving it back but have grown so fond of it that you never intend to give it back;
- You are hoping it has slipped my mind because you have no intention of giving it back;
- You think that the onus is upon me to ask for it back and my failure to do so means it is now yours;
- You feel that there is some unwritten rule that the failure to return, or ask for the return, of something borrowed over a specific period of time means it now belongs to the borrower.

Just so you know, you have my stuff and I want it back. It is mine and it is not yours. I should not have to ask you to return stuff that you borrowed from me. I extended to you a courtesy. You rewarded me by being ignorant and selfish. You have also put me in the awkward position of having to seek the return of something that you are acting like you own. I shouldn't have to do that.

I realize that this is now going to be a thing between us. You will say it is my fault. You will say I am making a huge deal out of nothing. You will seek the comfort of others and let them know how rude and awful I am. You are right. This is all my fault. It all started with me saying "YES". From now on, the answer is NO!

CHAPTER 24

POINTLESS CELL PHONE VOICE-MAIL MESSAGES

I don't know if your cell phone has this feature, but my cell phone provides a display that lets me know if someone has sent me a text, tried to call me or left me a voicemail message. It is actually an amazing technological innovation that tells me everything I need to know at a glance. I am betting that your cel phone also has this ability as well. I am also betting that you are aware of the fact that we both have the same amazing technology at our fingertips.

If you need to send me a quick message, a text is a great way to get the job done. If you don't have the ability to text, or just don't like to do it, you can always give me a call. If you are going to call me, I might not be able to answer the phone. There could be many reasons why this is the case. For instance, I might be charging my phone in another room; I suppose I might also be on another line and cannot excuse myself to speak with you at that time. I might also be brushing my teeth or otherwise disposed. Sadly, sometimes I just can't respond quickly enough when someone is looking to capture my attention by phone.

If you call and I don't answer, you should feel free to leave me a message. If you are going to do so, please make sure that the message has some meat to it. Please do not leave a message that sounds anything remotely close to the following: "hi, it is me, I just called to say hi. Give me a buzz when you get a chance".

Why am I opposed to such a message? Because it is not a message. It is a 'nothing burger'. The prompt on my display tells me the same thing.

It says (or means) the following: You called; and I should call you back when I get the chance. When you leave such a stupid and unnecessary voicemail message I know that: you called; and that you thought it would be fun for me have to go through the various prompts and channels necessary to hear your non-message.

I know you think that you have a special and soothing voice that the whole world loves to hear. Otherwise, why would you leave a message that says nothing that we can't figure out from our phone display? Are you insulted to know that people just delete your messages without listening to them because they know without listening to the message that there is nothing interesting to be learned? Can you imagine such telepathic brilliance?

Please understand I am not trying to insult or upset you. In fact, it would not surprise me that you are equally annoyed when people leave you non-messages. You just think that you are too special to treat others as you treat them. I hope you get my point here. If you don't, you aren't listening. And that is exactly what I am doing to you.

CHAPTER 25

BAD GIFTS

Did you ever wonder why it is that you don't get the kind of response you are hoping for when you give a gift to someone? You give them a household product, a piece of jewelry, or clothing and they just don't seem to be as appreciative as you might think to be appropriate under the circumstances. They don't ooo and ahhh. Or they make strange comments about a sweater like the stripes are very stripey. What if (God forbid) the gift you so painstakingly selected is nowhere to be found in their home because it has been re-gifted to someone else. How rude can people be?

But maybe they are not being rude at all. Maybe the problem is you. The truth of the matter is that you give terrible gifts. What you consider to be great thought on your end is actually perceived as "thoughtlessness" by the recipients of your intended generosity. How is this possible? I will tell you.

Whenever you give an unsolicited gift to someone you run the risk that it is not something they like or want. You place them in the awkward position of having to feign interest or appreciation. You wonder why you did not get an enthusiastic thank you. You tell the recipient how hard you worked at coming up with this special gift. You expect them to show great enthusiasm when it is killing them to do their very best acting job to thank you for such a stupid thing they did not want and will never use or wear.

Would you prefer that people were more honest about their true thoughts and stopped with the charade? Would you be okay with someone saying to you, "what the hell were you thinking?" How about if they said what they really felt–this gift sucks!!!

This may sound like an alien concept to you, but there is a really good chance that all gifts you give will be received with the greatest of appreciation if you actually give people something that they want. That is why there are bridal registries at high-end and most retail department stores. Brides (and to a lesser extent grooms are telling people what they want. Imagine that! I know this might take a little more effort than you might be able to muster, but why don't you try asking people for ideas and then—I am being totally serious here—actually getting the item that has been requested? If they want a specific pair of jeans, a toaster, or a washing machine of a specific capacity and color, get it. If they want cash or a gift card, give it.

Now you may not like this new-fangled concept of giving a gift. You may not want to be told what to do. Maybe that is your hang-up. You may not like the idea of writing a check or giving a gift card. It may be too impersonal, and that is just not your style. You are not alone in this world with that kind of thinking. You are also not alone when it comes to giving unwanted gifts. You just need to decide how alone you want to be.

CHAPTER 26
TALKING IN A MOVIE THEATRE

I have a special request for you; please be quiet when you are in a movie theatre. You can be with someone all day and barely say anything. Get you into a crowded movie theatre and you become a raging blabaholic.

For some reason you seem to think that a movie theatre is your own private family room. You make yourself comfortable by draping your feet over the seat in front of you. You throw used wrappers and boxes on the floor. And then, to top it all off, you proceed to strike up a conversation on a whole host of subjects. Even though someone is sitting right next to you, you speak to them in a loud voice. So loud that everyone is wishing and hoping you would shut the hell up.

I don't know about you, but I go to the movie theatre to watch a movie. Imagine that! I also like to watch the previews. Why? Because I get a tremendous opportunity to see some coming attractions that I might not otherwise have the good fortune of seeing anywhere else. They go through a lot of trouble to put the previews together and I don't want to disappoint the powers to be by missing even one second of their brilliant effort. For some reason you seem to think that previews are not important, and you can talk all the way through them. They may not be important to you, but I paid for the right to see them and you shouldn't spoil my opportunity to see and hear them. Nobody appointed you as judge and jury of the worthiness of previews. Since you don't hold a movie judgeship, you really need to give us all a break.

But the talking through previews issue is only the tip of the iceberg when it comes to you and your passion for gab. Is what you have to say really so important that it can't wait until the movie is over? And don't think for one second that whispering is somehow the better way to go. Shutting up completely is what I am looking for from you. When you whisper I can still hear you. It is annoying, and you are annoying. I am surprised you don't feel the penetrating eyes of all you offend trying to burn through your feeble brain.

I paid as much money to be in the theater as you did. I want my money's worth. I did not pay to hear a peep out of you. If I knew you were going to be there with a motor-mouth, I would have gone to another theatre or asked that they give you a muzzle. Why don't you do us all a favor and wait for the movie to come out on pay per view and watch it in your own home. We are all hoping you will give this serious consideration. Perhaps this is a bit too much to ask. Consideration is, after all, something you know nothing about.

CHAPTER 27

BAD HANDSHAKES

What is a good handshake? I would like to give you one right now, so the question is, what are you expecting? I think that most of us already know the answer to this question, but I am afraid that there are a number of people in this world (you among them) who just don't get it.

Have you ever gotten a wimpy handshake? What is that all about? Someone extends their hand to you (in a very reluctant manner) and ends up giving you a few fingers to grab onto that sneak their way back on out just as quickly as they possibly can. Did I say something to offend you? Is there something wrong with your hand? Is there something on it? Why don't you just be honest and tell me, "Look, I have some crap on my hand and you don't want to know where it came from". In that, case, no handshake is better than a wimpy one. Maybe I am better off just feeling a few fingers because if you have something you don't want me to see or feel, well, maybe I am just better off not knowing. Maybe you should give me a sign in advance of the wimpy handshake so that I can tell it is coming. In this way, I can at least decide as to whether yours is a hand worth shaking. How would you like it if I did the same thing to you? Maybe I should dispense with the few fingers routine and just wave my hand at you, thereby acknowledging your existence but not much else.

After all, and you must know this if you haven't already figured it out, when a person receives a wimpy handshake the receiver of the shake spends the next hour or so thinking about the character and morality (and overall personal hygiene) of the wimpy shaker (the W. S.) and they really have no more room in their brain to hear anything else the W. S. has to say.

Did they say something to me? I am not sure they did because they really aren't very deliberate in their hand shaking, so I would guess their personal messages are equally unclear. And, in case they didn't quite realize, the thought of the delivery of a wimpy handshake stays with the recipient for a good couple of years after the event, thereby negatively affecting a potentially wonderful relationship for no good reason. It is a very sad and troubling situation indeed and I would venture to guess that a W. S. would think twice about the quality of their shake if they ever really knew the ultimate consequences of their wimpitude.

Now, as I am sure you would expect, we have the other end of the spectrum, the Overly Hard Handshaker (the "Ouch"). What is it with these people? If you are 7 feet tall and have the hand the size of a steering wheel, I guess you probably think everyone else is a W. S. But you know, most of us are not of such large proportions and we expect to not be on our knees every time we extend our hand to make an introduction or renew an acquaintance. You really want to say something when they pour it on. How about telling them how impressed you are with the fact that they feel a need to kill you at first glance. Quite frankly, I am not impressed by an Ouch. I think they are trying to overcompensate for something and I really don't have the time or inclination to psychoanalyze their situation. I am pretty sure that Superman and Supergirl both go out of their way to power down their inner strength to extend a cordial howdy to any hand that is extended their way. They have nothing to prove. Obviously, the Ouch seems to think otherwise.

Handshaking does not need to be such an overwhelming problem. It is actually an activity that is very simple and easy to undertake. You just extend your right arm and hand and meet the right hand of the person you are addressing. If the person to whom your hand is extended does not return the favor, you put your hand down. If they do extend their hand, you know what to do. Or at least you should know what to do.

Since this simple act seems so perplexing to you, there may be some alternative that might be worth your consideration. You might want to consider stop shaking hands altogether and just start "Bowing" instead. It seems to work fairly well in a number of cultures, so maybe you should try it. There will have to be "Bowing lessons" so you can get it right. There certainly have to be rules as to frequency, duration, distance, rigidity and how low you must go. You definitely don't want to bow lower or longer than the person you are addressing. That is just flat out improper bowing. If you are going to head in that direction, it would be nice if you got it right. Show some consideration. Either that or don't be surprised when people avoid coming into contact with you. If you can't make proper introductions, you probably aren't worth meeting anyway.

CHAPTER 28

TOE-NAIL CLIPPINGS

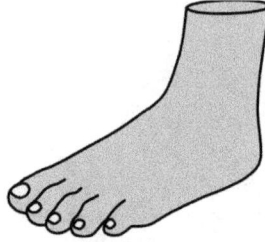

I like the fact that you think it is important to keep yourself well-groomed. You do a nice job of keeping your hair combed, and you seem to do all the right things that anyone would suggest or want for a person who is concerned about their self-image and the way in which they present themselves to the outside world. You also seem to spend quite a bit of time focusing on keeping your toenails cut and polished. It is just another part of the grooming process for you, but one that is of particular concern to me. It isn't the end result that causes me concern, it is the process you undertake to effectuate that result.

Let's take a look at how and where you clip your toenails. Sometimes it is at the side of the bed. Sometimes it is while watching television in the family room or while sitting on the toilet in the bathroom. Nail-cutting is a skilled procedure where you must be adept at removing just the right amount of nail and not digging down too deep for fear of biting off more than you can chew (ha-ha) or causing an infection. You seem to have that down pat.

What you seem to be having a problem with, and what bugs the hell out of me, is your careless disregard for where you deposit your clippings. They go every which where. They go on the floor, on the bed, on the couch; it really doesn't matter. At least to you that is the case. To me, it matters plenty. Nail clippings are the equivalent of tiny knives. They aren't quite as sharp, but they can pinch, prick and hurt when they catch you in the wrong position. Whatever they can do to me, they can also do to you. Whatever you drop has the potential of stabbing you or me (and anyone else for that matter). My problem is, therefore, your problem. It is a problem of your creation, and a potentially harmful or hurtful situation that is, by the way, totally uncool.

Even if you think I have blown this all out of proportion, why is it so hard for you to appreciate that this is disgusting, and a little courtesy might be in order? How would you like it if I flossed my teeth and left my food-laden string anywhere and everywhere? Do you think that is different? To me it isn't and that is the kind of revelation I am looking for you to both acknowledge and accept. How about including in your arsenal of cutting materials a paper towel where you carefully and gently place your blades of doom when the procedure is completed. I can appreciate that is somewhat of an inconvenience to you, but, trust me, it will be worth it to you, me, and many others in the end.

In case you think you are escaping unscathed with any mention of my issues associated with your fingernail clippings, think again. Fingernails are smaller, but the problem of your fingernail disposal is equally disgusting. If you don't like having to throw clippings away, then do what every hard-core and professional nail-biting person does; eat them. This makes for a more neat and tidy process and you can both groom and dine at the same time.

CHAPTER 29

CHEWING WITH YOUR MOUTH OPEN

I am sure you have heard it before, but I think it bears repeating; were you brought up in a barn? Do you know why people say that to you? It is because you chew with your mouth open like a cow and, of course, cows live in barns. I am pointing this out, so you can see the connection. I thought that the pinpoint specificity was necessary here because it seems to have eluded you. There is this concept of a barn and animals that live there. They conduct themselves in a certain manner. On a regular basis, you do what they do. If there were a vat of mud you would probably roll in it like a pig, but your bathing habits are the subject of another discussion.

You have an eating habit that is more than reminiscent of what is commonly known as "chewing of the cud". In the case of a cow, it is semi-degraded and regurgitated food. I am praying to God that is not what is going on in your case. If it is, you are a scientific marvel. Whether it is gum or a steak dinner that you are chewing, nobody really cares.

If a person is sitting next to you or directly across from you, they see your yap opening and closing like a finely-tuned motor. Sitting to the side of you they don't have the luxury of seeing the contents of your orifice. Having a direct shot of your mouthy treasure is another story. That unlucky person has the luxury of seeing exactly what you are working on. We prefer leaving it to our imagination. If it is food you are pummeling, then we do not need to see you rip, shred and mangle it before swallowing. We understand how the process works.

We actually have done that a few times ourselves.

Your gaping mouth issue is actually even worse than you think because sometimes you swallow some of what you eat and continue chewing the rest with your mouth open. This means that you, quite literally, "bite off more than you can chew". You are not eating properly. You are not taking proper-sized bites and you are proving to the world you don't know how to measure your food-to-mouth intake. Didn't they teach you that in kindergarten?

It would be greatly helpful if you could remember that the food you chew with your mouth open looks like garbage to everyone else. It is a poor eating habit and the sign of someone who prefers eating trash to traditional food products. If you are okay with that, rest assured that nobody else is. If you are going to eat with your mouth open, here is an idea, DON'T!!!

INAPPROPRIATE OR STRANGE BEHAVIOR

CHAPTER 30

ONE-UPSMANSHIP - KIDS

I think your children are totally amazing. Is that what you hoped I would say? I would think so, especially given the fact that you talk about them all the time. If I ask about them, you give me all the details. If I don't ask about them, you still find a way to weave them into a conversation. Don't get me wrong, they are lovely. I actually have no issue with them at all. It isn't that your children aren't deserving of praise. All kids are when they do something special. The problem isn't them. The problem is you.

You see, you seem to think your kids are God's gift to the world. They are incapable of doing anything wrong and anything they do is so amazing that everyone needs to hear about it. But it is even worse than that. For some reason you also think that everyone wants to know every little detail about everything that is going on with your children and you also think that everything they do is so amazing that it is truly beyond belief. You think that people genuinely care about their grades, their reports, their victories and successes. And not just in general; people want to know all the details, including pictures and video if available. You really could care less about anyone else's kids and, if you express interest, it is merely because you think it is expected of you as opposed to a matter for which you have genuine interest. Asking about others is just a ruse for opening the door so you can speak about your brood. You seem to think we are at some kind of Olympic kid-a-thon event with some very fierce competition. If I were ever to tell you anything about my own kids or the children belonging to someone else, you would see that as an opportunity to let the games begin. I find it better to say nothing than to give you the chance to do what I know you are dying to do as soon as you possibly can.

Do you know how many times you have one-upped the conversation? You don't even say: "That is so nice" or "that is amazing" to what anyone else might have to say about their kids. That is because you seem to think everyone else in this world is nothing compared to you and your lineage. And the sad thing is that nobody really cares about what you have to say. Nobody leaves a meeting with you feeling that they need to share your family news with anyone else. They leave feeling like they can't wait to get the hell away from you, and the sooner the better.

Perhaps you have nothing good or special to say about yourself and the only pleasure you get in life is derived through the accomplishments of your children. That is quite sad if it is true. But even if this premise is false, you really should be more considerate of others. You should appreciate that some people could care less about your brood and they have families as well that are just as near and dear to their hearts as yours are to you. You should adopt a 'don't ask, don't tell' policy. If people don't ask about your kids, they are begging you not to tell.

CHAPTER 31
TALKING BEHIND MY BACK

Did your mother ever tell you 'if you have nothing good to say about someone, say nothing'? If she did, chances are you either weren't listening, don't remember, or you never bothered to take this advice to heart.

I know for a fact that you talk behind my back. Our conversations always seem so upbeat and positive. Apparently, that is a ruse for how you really feel because what you tell me is nothing compared to what you seem to tell others about me and the way that you feel about me. You bad mouth me frequently. You are, for lack of a better phrase, "two-faced".

How is it possible that the person I thought I knew could be a totally different person when not in my company? What did I do to you that would cause you to speak so negatively about me? Why can't you tell me directly how you really feel? Why do I need to hear it all from others who, unlike you, appear to be my true friends?

And on top of all of this, how would you like it if the shoe were on the other foot? Since I am keenly aware that you talk negatively about me when I am not around, I want to let you in on a little secret. The people who let me in on the things you tell them behind my back are not your friends. I know about what you do because your so-called friends do not like what you do. You may think otherwise, but they are playing a game with you just like you are playing a game with me. The game is not 'poker' or 'old maid'. But it is most definitely one that will lead to something more akin to 'solitaire'. The real problem here is that we are both losing and that is not a good thing no matter how you slice it.

71

So, I am giving you fair warning that you need to stop this behind the back negativity. You are proving that our friendship is a sham and not worth pursuing. You have caused me to reconsider our relationship at every level. I hope that makes you as happy as I am in telling you my true feelings, so you are well aware of what I am seeing and how I feel about it. You might want to try this "truthfulness approach" yourself. Instead of telling tales about me to others, try telling them directly to the source. I am going to find about it anyway; because the people you thought to be your friends are actually my friends; and true friends don't talk behind the backs of people who are near and dear in their lives.

CHAPTER 32
AIR-KISSING

I really think that there needs to be a course taught in our institutions of higher learning on the proper manner for greeting a friend or loved one with a kiss to the cheek. I am not talking about intimate kissing. That is for another specialty course that is taught only at night. I am also not talking about kissing like you see in European countries; where people kiss the right and left cheek on purpose with no intent of actually making more than nominal physical contact to the facial area. I am speaking about greeting someone with whom there is more than a casual acquaintance or relationship. It is a situation where more than a hug would be considered good form, and proper social etiquette and a kiss to the cheek is either acceptable or expected.

I don't know why it is such a problem for you, but when you go to kiss people on the cheek, you turn your head to the side and end up kissing the air. You give an embrace, move your lips to the cheek and then turn your head. You turn it just enough to the left or right, to ensure that you make no contact with the skin. What you are doing is officially known as "air-kissing".

I think part of the problem is that people, like you, do not know which cheek to approach when going for the kiss. This is especially a problem if you are left-handed. Lefties always get things messed up. Nobody knows that better than me. There is so much work involved in figuring out which side to shoot for, the last step (the actual kiss) seems like an after-thought. And, by the way, please do not think you are alone. You are not the only person who seems to have this problem. I have been witnessing far too many people that hug and air-kiss someone who is hugging and air-kissing them right back. It is so very nice to see this incredibly synchronized and uncomfortable gesture.

For the record, you and everyone else who is guilty of air-kissing have no idea how stupid you look kissing the air. You seem to go all out in this hollow effort. I can actually hear the smack of your lips as you complete this awkward moment. I understand that this whole process can be difficult to undertake, but I don't think that is your problem. I truly believe that you do not like planting the kiss. You are so successful in not completing the mission that it seems to me that you really have no interest in making it happen. What I am trying to figure out is why you bother to add the kissing bit anyway. Why do you add that finishing touch when you clearly are not into it?

Maybe it should be a law that you must always go to the left (their right) when effectuating the hug/kiss. That will dispense with the awkwardness. Everyone will know what is expected of them if they care to do this properly. They can even have the option of heading to the left and not kissing at all. Just go for the hug. The kiss is optional. Kiss or don't kiss.

In your case I would not even bother kissing. You either don't do it correctly or you don't like doing it at all. Save yourself the effort and the embarrassment. Isn't that better than being well-known as a socially inappropriate kisser?

CHAPTER 33

MAKING OTHERS FEEL GUILTY

Here are some well-known sayings you may have heard or said yourself over the years: No, please don't bother, I will try and do it myself; Don't worry, I don't mind being alone; If you can't come, you can't come, but you will be sorely missed; Your brother and sister will be there; I don't need much, if it is not too much trouble; If you would reconsider I would appreciate it; after all, Lord knows how much more time I have on this earth.

There are countless other such sayings that I could have included. But I think you get my drift. All of these statements are things people say to make others feel guilty. Almost nobody is impervious to the power of these comments. That is why they are still used in every generation since the beginning of time.

The fact that people still use "guilt-laden" comments is a testament to their worth and value. The person seeking to have something done gets it done. They do so by manipulating the mind of the person to whom they are speaking. How cool is that? That is the purpose of laying on the guilt; and the more you do it, the more refined and skilled you become at attaining your goals and ambitions.

Some people use subtle comments to achieve desired results for mundane things. They might say, I hope you are going to change your underwear before you head out, in case you get into an accident." In this situation they are trying to help someone out. They are doing it for the person with the potentially messy underwear. They are not doing it for themselves. This is a guilt-laden comment bathed in kindness and wisdom. Imagine getting into a major car accident and having the ambulance driver, two policemen, a fireman and 17 eyewitnesses all looking at your soiled underwear. How guilty would you feel not having heeded this very practical advice?

In many families, there are relatives who do not stoop to subtle guilt. They believe in the "all or nothing" approach. They are in your face and mind like there is no tomorrow. Some are better at it than others. I am sure there is a book somewhere on the best ways to achieve success through guilt-laden comments. I know quite a few people who could have written that book. In fact, in my family, guilt is an art form. I can remember my grandmother asking me if I wanted a sandwich before heading out with my brother to mow her lawn. I told her "no". She asked again. I repeated my earlier refusal. In response she said the following: "I should die right now if you don't let me make you a sandwich." So, I did what anyone else would do, I had a sandwich, made with the special love that one can only get from the mother of one's mother or father. And, even more importantly, I also saved my grandmother's life.

Those of you who like or even love making others feel guilty take great pride in your ability to do so. If I told you it was resented, and it created deep-seeded psychological problems, you could probably care less. If I told you that it had the potential of limiting career opportunities, stifling relationships or ruining marriages, you wouldn't blink an eye. In fact, you would take no responsibility for any of that stuff because it was bound to happen anyway, and you are too nice to ever be considered at fault for something so horrific or troubling.

I think it is fair to say that life is tough enough as it is without the need to make it more complicated or difficult. I am trying to find the best way to communicate the fact that people who love to make you feel guilty, are evil and need to be avoided like the plague. I, along with most everybody else, need to find a way to make these doctors of guiltology feel guilty themselves. I am working on it. There has to be a way to get them to stop. There needs to be something concrete they can be shown to let them see why their approach is so awful. I am really having trouble with this one. The possible solutions are not easily forthcoming. How do you make guilty projecting people know how terrible and uncomfortable they make you feel? How do you make them feel badly about their actions? My sense is that you can't. They are immune. To them, it is sad that you might even consider it important to deal with this subject. It only proves a lack of maturity and lack of good manners. To the skilled purveyor of guilt, anyone thinking this way should be ashamed of themselves. My own penance for this transgression is obvious; I am now feeling guilty about being upset about people who make me feel guilty.

CHAPTER 34

BURPING

I know you are going to think that this is funny, but you have a disgusting habit of burping at the most inappropriate times and places. On top of that, you seem to think you are in some kind of a contest, the goal of which is to be the loudest and longest. If you think you will not have the stamina for a long one, you will definitely place greater emphasis on something loud that is unmistakable to anyone within a 30 to 40-foot perimeter of your burp echo chamber.

I must confess that I am sometimes caught off-guard by your burp-bursts and sometimes they can even be funny; however, for the most part, I am not amused. You think it is a joy to behold. A pee-in-your-pants event for which tickets should be sold. While you take great pride in your accomplishments, I am repulsed by you and want to know from which gutter you were dragged into society.

Aside from your rudeness, you are devoid of common courtesy. You don't even say "excuse me". There are 3 reasons for this: 1. You don't think it is any big deal; 2. You burp so often that it would be an imposition to continually have to say it; and 3. It is such a natural part of who you are and what you do that, to you, it would be like asking to be excused for clearing your throat. I would venture a guess that you are prouder of your burps than almost anything else that you do, with the exception, perhaps, of the killer gas from your derriere.

I want to go on record that I find your nasty habit gross and so does just about everyone else that I know within your immediate and not so immediate family. This is the same family that you see laughing when you decide to sound your horn. They aren't laughing with you; they are laughing at you. They would prefer not to be in your company and know that your burb-bombs must only be the tip of the iceberg of what clearly must be offensive behavior in a great many forms. Little to do they know.

Just keep doing what you are doing. Keep thinking it is no big deal and everyone thinks it is hysterical. Your judgment has always been clouded in this area and is unlikely to be cleared by these cold-hard facts. It is not your judgment that I want to be cleared anyway, it is the air. That can best be achieved if you would just shut your mouth and act like a normal human being.

I know it is a lot to ask, but you need to stop thinking you are a frat boy in college and start acting like a mature adult. Keep the following acronym in mind "KITY". Keep it to yourself. We don't want to hear it and, we don't want to be in the same room with you when you feel the need to gross us out. You may think that is just not who you are, and you do not want to repress your inner you. All I can say is that if repressing your inner gaseous emissions is going to kill you, it was nice knowing you.

CHAPTER 35
INAPPROPRIATE KISSING ON THE LIPS

In America, it seems to be common for very young children to kiss their parents on the lips. But, at some point in their development, the rules of lip-kissing change. I am not sure if it is a specific age or if it is gender-dependent. There does not seem to be any statutory enactments on this subject, so that is of no help either. Believe me, I checked.

When you are older and in love, lip-kissing comes back in style. In fact, it is taken to all-new and very exciting heights. Some heights are even higher than others. Sometimes, of course, more than lips get into the action. Exactly what age is appropriate for this lip-kissing action to begin seems to be as unclear as when it is not appropriate for young people to lip-kiss parents. Some still do, regardless of age. But others may find that a bit out of sorts and not their cup of tea.

So, the rules on lip-kissing are not necessarily written in stone. There is no rhyme or reason, but there are some general taboos and some circumstances where people are likely to turn up their noses or talk behind the backs of others. And you know what I am talking about and you know who you are. Although there are no truly hard and fast rules on the subject, there is one RULE that you seem to not appreciate. Perhaps when the rule was being discussed you thought they said 'fuel' and went to get gas for your car. The rule is actually quite simple: "you don't kiss on the lips a married man or woman, who is otherwise spoken for."

I have a question for you. What in the hell is the matter with you? Are you not getting enough at home? Are you getting your jollies elsewhere by finding opportunities to engage hitched acquaintances with lip locks? Do you attend certain social gatherings searching for victims, so that you can satisfy your vice? Do you select victims like a heat-seeking missile and position yourself for a planned approach?

Perhaps it never occurred to you how awkward it is for the person who has sought to avoid your oral fixation. They may seek to head in the opposite direction knowing that a situation is about to occur that will leave them embarrassed or wondering what is wrong with you. Some may actually pop a breath mint in advance of your approach. I guess for them this is really not a problem at all. But it may be an issue for their significant other; or your significant other; all of who might contemplate remedying the situation, especially if they were to become aware of your inappropriate activity.

I suppose this isn't the worst thing you could do in life in the scheme of things. After all, it is only a kiss. You approach someone, and they turn their head to the side and you instinctively head in the direction you know they are turning so you can connect with some nice, warm lips. For you it is a science. For them, it is usually quite awkward. Maybe you never really think anything of it. Maybe you need to think again. This is some really weird and socially inappropriate behavior. I am calling you out on it. Keep your lips to yourself. If they feel the need to wander, don't be surprised if someone decides to slap the face that approaches places where it clearly doesn't belong.

PERSONAL PROBLEMS

CHAPTER 36

BAD FACIAL PLASTIC SURGERY

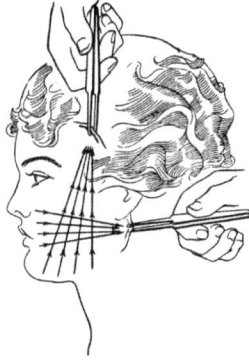

There are many well-known celebrities who have had plastic surgery on their face. In some instances, you can't quite tell for sure. You might suspect that is the case; however, unless they come out and say it is true, you really don't know. You find yourself wondering. You might even casually make mention of it to someone you know. There is a great deal of speculation that ensues, but nothing is definitively determined, and life goes on with another mystery of the universe left for others to solve.

Then there are the celebrities who have definitely had something done to them. You can see it in the "before and after" pictures. You can also tell by just looking at them. Something is up. It doesn't look real. You don't need to be a rocket scientist to be able to tell that this looks messed up, big time. The wrinkles are gone, and things look too tight. There is a pronounced puffiness that wasn't there before. And let's not forget about the lips. They now have an effect that a clown would envy. Did they actually pay someone to do that?

And that, my friend, is now you. Everywhere you go, whether you know it or not, people are talking about you. Maybe that was your plan. Maybe you were hoping they would be speaking about how young you now look. I am sorry to have to tell you that your grand plan has backfired, big-time. What they are saying is anything other than what you hoped to be the case. You just better double check and see if your plastic surgeon has good malpractice insurance because that is what we are looking at here.

I realize this all sounds cruel and hurtful, but what did you expect? You couldn't leave well enough alone? Did you want honesty or dishonesty? Is there anyone in your circle of "real friends "or "caring family members" who have actually told you that you look good? If that is the case, they are not your friends or loving family. Get them all out of your life as quickly as you possibly can.

There is an old saying that "one should not mess with mother nature." In this case we are not looking at anything that even remotely appears to be natural. It is, however, a mess. You should seriously consider getting your situation fixed. I hope you are not too late. You might want to check references this time because, obviously, that was something that was sorely lacking when you went under the knife for your current Halloween facial.

CHAPTER 37
YOU BET YOUR ASS

I don't know if you realize it, but you really do not take yourself very seriously or have great confidence in yourself. While you might beg to differ, there is one little thing that you say, over and over again, that lends credence to my observation.

Whenever I or anyone else push you a bit on your level of certainty and self-assuredness on a particular topic, instead of standing tall in the saddle and speaking with conviction, you frequently like to wager the odds associated with your position. The crazy thing about this wager is that you put nothing at risk. Instead, your common refrain is "you bet your ass". "Are you going to the wedding? You bet your ass." "Did you make reservations? You bet your ass." I want you to know I take issue with this response and I want to be clear that your comment is never well received.

First and foremost, it is obvious that you don't seriously consider what you are saying when you make this silly comment. It is somewhat of a popular refrain, but the key here is that you are placing the odds of you being right on my ass. Why in the hell would you do that? Why is my ass being placed at risk when I am not the one who is defending a situation or proposition for which asses are part of the solution?

Secondly, why does this so quickly become about me? It should start and end with you. If you believe in something, then you should buy into it wholly and unconditionally and with every fiber of your being and body parts. If you want to risk anything associated with a position that you are taking, that is your deal. That is totally up to you. If you want me to buy in or take some risk, ask me. I will let you know where I stand or whether I think you are nuttier than a Snicker's bar.

Do not drop these clichés to justify or give credence to your dedication to a position, philosophy, stance, direction, attitude or plan. It means nothing. It shifts the burden from one of certainty to a focus on my body where it most definitely does not belong. If you mean what you say, and you really want to give emphasis to your level of seriousness, then you need to drop me from the conversation and have the courage of your convictions and place your ass squarely on the line. The bottom line is this, if you mean what you say, "bet your own ass, not mine".

CHAPTER 38

PICKY DINERS

    I am going to tell you something that you already know; you are a picky dining companion. You think the fact that you know makes it okay that you qualify for this classification. You think that, when it comes to spending money, it is perfectly okay to be overly choosy. Trust me, it isn't okay. It is annoying as hell. You think that you should be able to have your dining experience exactly the way you like it, regardless who is paying for it. To that I say, great; as long as I am not around and as long as I don't have to suffer through what I know will be a totally uncomfortable experience.

    Dining with you means any one or more of the following will likely be said, at some point, to me, another dining companion, or to a member of the waitstaff at a restaurant:

- I would like to sit in a booth
- Not this booth, the other one
- Not this room, the other one
- I don't like this chair
- It is too drafty
- It is too hot in here
- It is too cold in here
- It is too dark
- It is too bright
- I liked the old décor better
- It is too noisy
- There are too many menu choices, I can't make a decision
- There aren't enough menu choices, we should go elsewhere

- Nothing looks good on the menu
- I want the salad, but I don't want the croutons or the tomatoes. I would like extra cucumbers, and could you add a scrambled egg and bacon bits
- Do you have some other greens besides lettuce?
- I want my dressing on the side
- I don't like this dressing, I would like a few more dressing choices to taste
- I would like my entrée on a separate plate from the rest of my meal
- I like my fries extra hot, don't bring them to me if they are just warm
- I want the sauce on the side and on a separate plate
- These eggs are too runny
- These eggs are too well done
- I want butter on my toast, but not too much
- I like my toast burnt
- This toast is burnt
- I would like a cheeseburger without the cheese and without the bun – I want 3 slices of tomato and no lettuce – I want the onions, but I want them cooked
- I want tomatoes, but they need to be really deep red
- I want no pickles
- I want extra pickles
- I want the soup – extra hot and with extra stock – less broth – more of the good stuff
- This food is cold
- This food is literally freezing
- I want it cooked medium rare, but more rare than medium
- I want it well done, but not too well-done
- It is too well-done
- I don't like my steak; can I have the chicken?
- I don't like the sauce; can I get it re-done without the sauce?
- I don't like it; can I get a salad instead?
- I would like a glass of soda with no ice
- I would like ice on the side
- I would like some vegetables that you used to serve a year ago
- I don't like your desserts, what do you have that is not on the menu?
- I would like decaf with 1% milk – not skim, regular, or half and half

Just once, I am begging you, is it possible for you to join me at an eating establishment for a normal dining experience? Just once could you order something off the menu and say that you want it just the way it is described? Is that even remotely possible? Do you see something on a menu and think about how you would build it differently? Is that what goes on inside your head? If so, get it out. Please do so immediately because I can't stand it. I hate suffering through it. Also, when you get whatever they bring, I want you to say it is perfect, even if it kills you and you are going to drop dead right there on the spot.

The easy way around this is to always order in. That way I will be less embarrassed by what will most assuredly go on in a public establishment. It will be a less cringe-worthy experience for me. For you, it will be no big deal. You will get your meal exactly the way you like it and I won't have to suffer the embarrassment of your picky, dining, crazy shenanigans.

CHAPTER 39

BAD BREATH

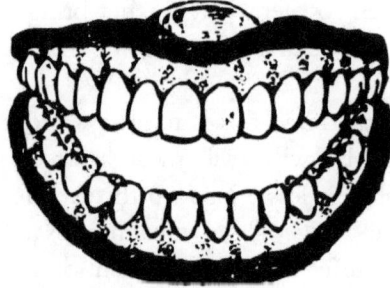

I am going to tell you something that you should already know. You have bad breath. Let's call it halitosis. That sounds more scientific and less crass. It doesn't change the facts. It just makes reality sound more clinical and easy to deal with. Regardless what you call it, the reality is this: you have a situation that necessitates a significant widening of the personal space between you and anybody else with whom you might come into contact.

When I say that you have bad breath I do not mean that it is not pleasant. Getting stung by a mosquito is not pleasant. In your case we are talking about extremely offensive and gag-worthy odor. We are talking about something so bad that we would all be better off if you considered wearing Limburger cheese perfume. Is there any other way to be more blunt and honest?

Quite frankly, I am surprised you are not aware that you have a problem. Do you not see people recoil in horror when you are speaking to them upfront and close? How is it possible that nobody has ever mentioned this to you? Perhaps they have, and you have either brushed off the comment or forgotten about it. Brushing it off is not the way to go. Forgetting it is really not possible. The stench is truly unforgettable.

Maybe you do have some basic appreciation for your situation. Perhaps you use mouth wash, brush frequently and carry some tic tacs with you for occasional use. Whatever you are doing, please understand this: it isn't working. I don't know if you need to see a doctor, change your eating habits or have a combination of cinnamon Altoid's and Wrigley's

Spearmint Gum implanted into your mouth. But, for God's sake, please do something.

Rest assured that, whatever you decide to do, the benefit will be much less for you than it will be for the rest of us. Obviously, you do not seem to have a problem going through life with "stinky-mouth". It does not affect your ability to drive, watch television or play sports. It is not debilitating to your life. But doing nothing is a very selfish act on your part.

Most everything you do requires that you come into contact with other people. For the sake of our planet and the people who live there, please do something about your problem. I am begging you! We want what you want. We want to be happy. For the most part, we are; unless and until you open your mouth.

CHAPTER 40

YOUR PERFUME REEKS

I don't think I have to tell you how special you are. You are one of a kind. But not for the reasons you might suspect. The thing that makes you so special is the fact that you stink. Not like a foul odor that would be more akin to sewage. But more like a stinging and horrific scent that brings tears to my eyes and the eyes of everyone else around you. You may not have noticed, and you may not believe this to at all be the case, but, trust me, it is all true.

My discontent is all attributable to the perfume or cologne that you wear. For you it is not something you delicately dab on key parts of your body. It is more like lotion that you rub all over the place. Maybe that sounds like an exaggeration, but your smell suggests otherwise.

People can tell you are coming from miles away. And they also know that you have been around for hours long after you are gone. Your scent lingers, but not in a way that is the least bit pleasing. Your odor suffocates anything and everyone you touch. If you hold a baby, it will be on their clothing and in their crib when they get home. If you sit on a couch, the smell will find its way on to the derriere of the next person who sits there. It will eventually wind up in their closet. You follow people everywhere they go without having to go anywhere yourself.

I would ask you to let me know the name of the perfume or cologne you are using. You might mistake the request for an affirmation of the wonderful delight you are wearing. Again, that would most definitely not be the case. I want to write the manufacturer and demand that they refuse to sell their product to you or change their product design to limit applications. Maybe it is a bad mixture, or you don't know how to wear it with dignity. I am not willing to take the chance that it is the latter. If you don't know how to properly use it, maybe it must be eradicated from the face of the earth.

Hopefully you are not amused by these sad facts. Perhaps you might see this as an opportunity to do something about this situation for the benefit of every human being and animal that comes into contact with you. If you ask someone if you have overdone it with your perfume or cologne application, please do not believe them if they say no. Whatever you believe to be the appropriate amount, you are wrong. Always do less. The less the merrier.

CHAPTER 41

YOUR SINGING IS AWFUL

Do you like to sing in the shower? You turn on the hot water, get in and a switch goes off in your head. You feel relaxed and uninhibited. You have this warm feeling all over you and the happiness it brings you causes you to belt out one of your favorite tunes. I am really happy that you feel so care-free at that special moment of time. But I want you to know that this happiness is not overwhelming on my end. I am happy for you, but I am not very happy for me. Why? Because your singing is God-awful.

I am actually surprised you don't know how bad you sound. You are either tone deaf or you just don't care. I am not sure which, but I guess that is not important. What is important is that you come to grips with this very important fact.

As much as I hate having to discuss your singing atrocities, I cannot believe that there haven't been many clues for you to absorb after all of these years. Were you ever in a choir? Were you given the lead, asked to stand in the back row or was your sole duty handing out lyric sheets? If you hear a song on the radio and start singing, do others try to sing louder to drown you out or do they ask you to change the station? If you are singing along with others in a public place, such as a church or at your favorite sports facility, do people look over at you with a look of pain on their faces? You see what I mean? These are clues. You need to get one.

Please do not be mad at me for telling you something you should have already known. In fact, instead of being mad at me, I want you to know that I am mad at you. Why shouldn't I be? You are the worst singer on the planet. Your singing voice is worse than a symphony of 100 people running their nails along a blackboard. Every lyricist and singer who ever lived is insulted that you would ever consider singing their song in any way other than within the innermost recesses of your mind.

You have been hurting me and countless others for years with your terrible voice. The bottom line is this; If you feel the urge to sing, suppress it. Do something else. Watch a movie. Learn how to hum. Become a professional hummer. Do nothing more. If you are inclined to sing, DON'T!

CHAPTER 42
SO MUCH TO DO, SO LITTLE TIME

You have to be the busiest person I have ever met. Whenever I give you a call, you always are in a rush to go here or there. You always seem to be on a mission. There just doesn't seem to be enough time in the day for you to accomplish all the things you need to do. You are truly a marvel.

You probably think that I feel sorry for you and the hectic schedule you keep. You also probably think that all of your friends feel the same way. You must also think that we all shake our heads in disbelief that anyone could do so much over the course of a day, week or month. Perhaps you think we feel for what is obviously a miserable and hectic life and lifestyle. Maybe we are grateful that our lives are nothing like yours. But, no matter how you look at it, surely we must all believe that you are truly an impressive person, given all that you are able to accomplish over so little time.

Trust me when I tell you, nobody marvels at anything you do. Nobody feels sorry for you in any meaningful way. But we all do feel sorry about this: it is such a shame that you are so scatterbrained that you cannot accomplish daily tasks like everyone else.

Whenever I or anyone else asks for your help with a project or task, you are always too busy for us. We are never too busy for you. If you need us, we are always there. When we need you, you are nowhere to be found. Have you ever stopped to think about that? Does this seem fair to you? Do you acknowledge this but mentally excuse yourself because of everything you have to do? Does this resonate with you or, are you caught off-guard by this and need to add it as another task to consider along with all the other things that seem to keep you so incredibly busy day-in and day-out?

This may come as a surprise to you, but we all have busy lives as well. I know that is hard for you to believe. Nobody could possibly be as busy as you think you are. Did you do some mathematical calculations as to our lifestyle requirements and yours and determine that you win the burden of life award? Do you know how annoying it is to ask someone if they can do something for you, but be told they can't because they are planning something that is months away and they can't focus with all that is on their mind. Holy mackerel! It is a wonder you can breathe with all you have going on. So, what are you doing that is so time-consuming? Are you planning a vacation 3 months from now and need to buy a new pair of goggles and book a rental car? That is amazing. Nobody could possibly do all of that in 3 months and still brush their teeth every day. If I were you, I might forego truth brushing for a while just to minimize the overwhelming anxiety that you must be experiencing. Do you get the picture?! Does any of this resonate with you?

Listen closely; you need to get your act together. You need to stop whining and bitching about all of your problems and live a more normal life. If you really have too much going on, then you need to cut some things out. The cooking class, snake charming, string untangling and the "go fish" weekly card game may need to go. I realize you will miss them, but you and everyone else will be better off for it. You will be much less stressed out and family members and friends will get along with you a whole lot better. You will actually be a fun person. You will be more caring, understanding and helpful toward others beyond your current chaotic lifestyle. This is a chaos that you created, allowed to be created or isn't nearly as bad as you make it out to be. Do something about this. Do it now. And do not, by the way, react to all of this by saying what I fully expect you to say: "I can't do as you ask because, given my current lifestyle, the possibility of fixing my life does not fit into my schedule.

CHAPTER 43
CLEAN OUT YOUR EARS

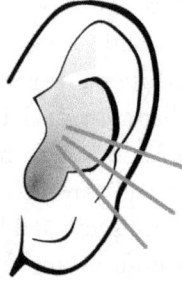

We have two problems between us. The first is the arguments we get into because of things you say I don't tell you. The second involves the fact that I do not communicate well. I realize these are my problems. I wish I could do better. Unfortunately, I am afraid that will never happen, and we are destined to live with this situation that sometimes seems to overwhelm our relationship. It may sadden you to learn of my resolve, but I feel this is best. It is a problem without a solution on my end. There is one on yours - 'clean out your damn ears'.

You have no idea how frustrating it is to me when you say that I never told you something that I am certain I did. You tell me that you are sure I am wrong. You tell me I am getting old and my memory isn't what it used to be. You occasionally feel sorry for my acute memory loss. I cannot quibble with the possibility that I might forget a few things, here and there. I might even have thought I told you something and didn't because I told so many people that I thought you were included in the group. But the frequency with which you scold me for keeping you in the dark is too great to be fact. I am not losing my mind. You have lost your ability to hear.

Sometimes you say, "oh yeah, I remember", after I remind you that this isn't the first time I am telling you about something. You are not fooling anyone if you think, for even one second, that I believe it is all coming back to you. You are not re-remembering. You did not mis-remember. You either heard it all wrong the first time or you simply never heard it at all. It is even possible that you heard it differently. For example, is it possible that I did not say "I am going to the rifle range," and was actually saying "I am taking my car for an oil change"?

I can't be the only person who suffers because of your hearing issues. It must also happen for other people you relate to on a daily basis. They probably have to develop strategies to compensate for your shortcomings. I have had to do that far too frequently. When you tell me I never told you something or I told you something differently, you are calling me a liar. You may not be using those words, exactly, but that is what it means. I don't like being called a liar. I would prefer that you listened when I speak to you and that I be extended the same courtesy that you expect when you speak to me.

Maybe you actually have a serious issue that goes well beyond cleaning out your ears. Maybe you need hearing aids and are loathing to join others who have reluctantly succumbed to a lifetime of battery replacements. I can appreciate why you might feel that way. I would probably have the same sentiment if the shoe were on the other foot. But, since it is not, I need you to either do something about your problem or cut me some slack. Just to be clear, I did not just ask you 'if you would get me a snack'.

CHAPTER 44

BAD TOUPEES

Can you imagine a 98-year-old man with a full head of jet black hair? I think you would agree that would look quite strange. How about an 80-year-old man with the same look? That really wouldn't cut it either. As you make your way down the old to young ladder you will eventually come to an age bracket where a full head of jet black hair looks appropriate. As you consider all the possibilities, perhaps you might also be wondering where your situation falls on the reasonableness spectrum. Here is the thing, you don't.

You have a look that is way out of sorts. Your hairdo does not go with your face or age. That is because you have no hairdo. You have a 'hair-don't'. You wear a toupee. It is someone else's version of a hairdo. I am not an expert on this subject, but I think the key to having a toupee is to fool people into believing it is your real hair. Trust me when I tell you, we are nobody's fool. You are wearing something that belongs to someone else. It might even belong to a different species.

Some people allow their hair to age gracefully. Some shave their head at an early age when there is no hair loss issue at all. They simply like the look. There are other people who have gotten hair implants and transplants. Some have dabbled in the world of hair growth products. But you have done none of these things. You have gone for a hair strategy that says the following: *"I care so strongly about the way that I look that I am going to go the cheap route and send a clear message that I don't care about the way that I look."*

I am only trying to help you by pointing out how your appearance is viewed by the rest of the world. I mean no harm. I also want you to know that you would look 100% better without that dust collector on your head. Maybe you might want to consider going au naturale. Yes, it will take some getting used to. But, in a short period of time, it will become the new you that is embraced by one and all.

If you would prefer to continue to go the way of the toupee, at least get a good one. Get something that seems age appropriate that is also a good fit. If you don't change your hair strategy, 2 things are going to happen: 1) people will talk about you behind your back; and 2) people will go on thinking that your toupee looks as good on you as 'socks on a rooster'.

CHAPTER 45

YOU STINK

I know you don't realize it, but you stink. I am not talking about an overpowering floral scent or something about your perfume or cologne that is a bit too much. I am also not talking about something a little unpleasant when you turn this way or that or when you raise your arms. I am not talking about any of that at all.

I have to be honest with you that I am not at all happy about having to be the bearer of these unpleasant tidings. Of all the things that I or anyone else could say about or to anyone, this is about as bad as it can get. And, when I say you stink, I am being kind. What I really mean is that you exude a foul and nasty odor that would cause anyone to run for the hills. It is the kind of stench that the federal government typically regulates. To put it in terms that are without ambiguity, the smell is so bad that, quite frankly, (and pardon my French) it would knock a buzzard off a shit wagon.

I am hoping that you were unaware of the fact that you have a gamey scent about you and that you need to take corrective action. Maybe you wish that you were aware of this long-ago and are livid with the possibility that I, as well as your friends and loved ones, have felt this way for some time and didn't extend to you the courtesy of giving you a clue. Don't be too hard on us as I am sure you can appreciate how hard it is to bring this up. And don't be surprised that, if you do mention it, you might learn that we left you clues all over the place. We wouldn't let you near certain places; we wouldn't invite you to certain events; we would never consider borrowing any of your clothing; and we wouldn't use your towels or sit on your couch, etc., etc., etc., etc. You get the point.

But what if you were aware of this issue and thought you were doing something about it? Now that would be pretty bad. If that were the case, guess what? Your efforts have fallen well-short of the mark. Your corrective action has not corrected a damn thing. Please try again. Not just please, pretty please!

Worst of all, what if now that you know, you don't care? You intend to do nothing. What if, as far as you are concerned, everyone can suffer? If they don't want to be in your company, that is fine with you. I am hoping this is not the case. I am hoping, in fact, praying, that you do not cop an attitude about this and you decide to do something about your stench. I do not want to have to take my car to the car wash every time you go for a ride. I do not want to have to wash my clothes every time they come into contact with you. For the love of God, please do something about this. Until you do, you now have a better understanding as to why there is a mass exodus of people when you show up. Obviously, they can't all have a dentist appointment at the same time and every time you are in their company.

SOCIAL CONSCIOUSNESS

CHAPTER 46

I COULD CARE LESS HOW YOU ARE DOING

Hello, how are you? How are you and the family doing? Better yet, as they say in various parts of New York and Rhode Island, "how ya doin?" Have you ever said any of these things to someone? Has anyone ever said them to you?

You may not realize it, but you ask this question of me and just about everyone else you know every time you see me and them. You probably think nothing of it. You may even think it is expected that you make this inquiry. You can take some comfort in knowing most people do just like you. They ask this same question.

Truth be told, "How are you doing" is often a meaningless interchange between people. Very little consideration is given toward what should be a very thoughtful and important aspect of basic human interaction. So, here is what I want to know; when you ask someone how they are doing, do you really want to know the answer? And when it is asked of you, does the person doing the asking really give a damn? The answer to my question is quite obvious, if you are really being honest about your true feelings on this subject.

Many years ago, I was with my grandfather when he met up with an old friend. He was asked how he was doing. He proceeded to answer the question in great detail. He told his friend about his recent car accident and the problems he was experiencing with his prostate. I am sure there were other wonderful things that were discussed, but I don't remember.

What I do remember was telling my grandfather after the guy left that I could not believe that he went into such a long descriptive narrative about his various troubles. I said his friend did not really care to know all about that stuff. And do you know what he said to me? Well, if he didn't want to know, he shouldn't have asked.

The truth of the matter is that, for the most part, nobody really wants to know anything negative when they ask; "how are you doing?" You say that you want to know, but you really don't. You hope that people like me will say; "fine thanks, and you?" In fact, most people say just that without even thinking. They most often do not tell you the truth. They could be in unbelievable pain with a flare-up of hemorrhoids. A loved one may be near death. They could have lost a check for $6,838 on the job. But even though all of these troubling things may be ongoing in a person's life, you will probably never know; and you may not be interested in knowing anyway.

Sometimes the response to "how are you doing" might be "you don't want to know". When we hear that, we are grateful that they do not elaborate, and we frequently do not ask for the details. We should, but we don't. Why? Because we don't really care. You know that I am right about this. For the most part, the answer to this innocent question is "great" or "fine", which, as we all know, is a complete fabrication of the truth. It has gotten to the point that "how are you doing" is just filler words for a pleasantry with no real meaning or purpose other to make small talk; and that is a shame.

My grandfather may have gotten it right all along. In his honor I have decided to mount a one-person war on this customary pleasantry. I hope you will join me in this effort. When I am asked "how I am doing?" I am going to answer truthfully. If I have a stomach ache, you are going to hear about it. If I cut myself shaving, you will get the bloody details. If I do not get enough raisins in my box of raisin bran, you will learn about that as well. If you ask, be prepared for an honest answer that includes some positive but a lot of negative things that have happened to me, no matter how mundane. I am hopeful that the result of my new campaign will be a more honest discussion with family members and friends. It may also result in less communication from people who really could care less about my sudden bout of truthfulness. I am both sorry and happy to say that my newfound honesty will most likely result in shorter conversations with much less meaningless chit-chat.

I think I am onto something here. We might all benefit from my new approach to basic human interaction. I will truthfully answer the question that you and most other people don't even realize you are asking. You are now going to know how I am doing in every way imaginable. This has been a long time in coming and I am anxious to get started. And I have also decided that, unless I really want to know how a person is doing, I am going to stop asking. Please do not be offended if I don't ask how you are. If I do not ask for this information, but it is offered without prompting, I might have to do something about that. I might stop people in their tracks and tell them; "I am not interested and, quite frankly, I really could care less how you are doing."

CHAPTER 47

BAD WAITERS AND WAITRESSES

Everyone wants a monetary tip for just about anything and, in some cases, for doing nothing at all. Generally speaking, it seems like a good idea to give a tip to someone in the service industry who has performed a service. We all do it for the most part. Well, at least most of us do it. Some people are more generous than others. If they are rich, they can afford to be a bit more generous and, even if they are not, they certainly don't want to be known as a cheapskate at their favorite restaurant.

But regardless of whether a diner is rich or not as well off, a tip should be given to someone who deserves one. Why? Because it is expected and, until the economics of dining changes, it is the way it is.

While the idea of giving a tip is important, the notion that one is always deserved is another thing entirely. The expectancy of a tip, regardless of whether it is deserved seems to be lost on some people in the service industry. You would be one of these people. Why do we give tips in the first place? Someone told me a long time ago that the word "TIPS" is an acronym for "To Insure Prompt Service". I am not going out on a limb to suggest that prompt service should also include good service. This is not rocket science. If you give good and prompt service, you should get a decent tip. A nice smile and a friendly personality are also considered a nice touch. If you don't get such service and friendliness, you deserve less; or, depending upon how badly you perform, I suppose you deserve nothing at all.

For you, a decent tip is expected, regardless of the job you do. If you go to a bad play or concert, would you expect people to stand up and clap and cheer if the performance was mediocre or substandard? A tip is like an ovation. The better the performance, the louder the ovation. If you are truly amazing, you will get a standing ovation in the form of a great tip. If you aren't very good, you should expect to receive something that reflects that reality. The problem is when you think you are great and when you obviously are not. Your tips should reflect performance. When you stink, tips should reflect stinkiness. When you are great, and you are left with a poor tip, it might be the diner is just a cheapskate or mathematically challenged. That is indeed unfortunate, and you are not to be blamed for such stupidity.

Good waiters and waitresses deserve great tips. Of that there is no doubt. But I am not talking about them. I am addressing those instances when the result is a just and fair reflection of a job performance that is something less than what one thought to be deserved. The recipient of the poor tip will think it is the customer who has failed to appropriately compensate their brilliance. The patron is clearly suggesting otherwise and for obviously good reason.

Here is a list of 7 things that you might want to consider changing if you are a waiter or a waitress who makes a living providing a service that, for the most part, is reliant upon TIPS and the generosity of others.

1. It isn't them, it is you. You are not very good at what you do. Keep doing what you do. You will continue to get your mediocre reward.

2. Please take your sweet time coming to my table and asking me if I want a drink. I just love that. Better yet, while you see me staring at you and hoping you are going to come to my table please go to the table next to mine and start cleaning up the mess left by the patron who just walked out the door.

3. Please do not smile or seem friendly in any way. It makes me sad when you do and reminds me why I needed that drink in the first place.

4. If my order is going to take a while longer than expected, please do not let me know. Let me sit in my misery thinking that you just don't care or, better yet, that my order was eaten by some other fool who came in after me.

5. When you bring me my order, please do not ask me if there is anything else that I need. Assume you are like God and it isn't possible that you could have forgotten anything or that I could possibly want for anything more than you have so graciously provided before me.

6. After you bring me my order, please do not check up on me to see if everything is okay. You really should not even feign interest. I can see right through you, so don't even bother.

7. And finally, if I tell you there is something wrong with my order or the way it is prepared, please argue with me. Please tell me I don't know what I am talking about. Please don't tell your manager about my level of dissatisfaction and, above all, please do not try to rectify the situation by arranging for a credit or some type of offset from my bill.

If you are not the type of person who does any or all of these things, you are probably already richly rewarded and deservedly so. If you do any or all of these things you can be assured of nothing. You will not receive a rousing ovation or monetary riches beyond your wildest dreams. People will not come into your establishment looking for you and hoping that you will give another performance for their continuing consternation, aggravation, and immense displeasure.

CHAPTER 48

UNINTELLIGIBLE PHONE MESSAGES

The other day I was checking my phone messages and I noticed that I received a call from someone whose number I did not recognize. So, I played the message and a couple of things became painfully obvious; I did not understand the name and number that they left.

When someone quickly leaves a message, without great thought as to clearly leaving their content and/or contact information, they cause the message recipient to replay the message. That is, of course, if the recipient cares enough to find out what they did not understand at the first pass. The person doing the replaying has paper and pen in hand waiting to get to the part of the message where the contact info was spoken. Sometimes they miss it and have to start all over again. When they hear it, they write it down; or they write down what they hear, or what they think they hear. Maybe they need to replay the message a number of times in order to get all the info. And even after that, they still might not be certain that they have written down everything correctly. In case you didn't know, dear message-leaver, you are being silently cursed by the person you initially called. Why? Because you leave unintelligible phone messages.

I suppose we could press redial and call the number of the person who left the message. If you are a lazy person you might not see it as being worth the effort. What if the call was important, but it was an 800 number? What if the number was 'blocked'? In either case, pushing redial would serve no purpose. What if the number goes to a large office and the company receptionist does not recognize the convoluted name of the person to whom you wish to be connected? Then it would be almost impossible to speak with the person who left the message.

As a result of a poorly left message, the recipient is potentially left clueless as to the true nature of the call and how to make contact with the caller. The inarticulate caller may be wrongfully assuming that the recipient of their poorly left message could care less about them and the recipient may be thinking the exact same thing. In the case of potential business opportunities, someone who is reaching out from a poorly left phone message may now be taking their business elsewhere. What kind of a heart attack might you have if you missed the important contact info for the following message: "Hi, I am calling to order 25 rocket ships. I am willing to proceed with you if you could cut your price to $991,000,000 apiece. I have another quote from a competitor and will be making my decision today at 5 PM. Please let me hear from you before then so I can seriously consider doing business with your company."

Many of the problems we have in this world are attributable to poor communications. Every one of us can do our part to improve this sad state of our world. This may be a little difficult for you to comprehend, much less do, but please consider the following when leaving a voice mail message: 1. Speak slowly, succinctly, and clearly; 2. When leaving your name, spell it. You might even consider making a joke of it. My name is Mark (rhymes with shark) Petrasinocchio (rhymes with "kleptrasinocchio"); and 3. State your phone number and then (this next part is so amazing I have Goosebumps), say it again.

I can't speak for the rest of mankind, but I know that, if I want someone to know my name and number, I want to make sure that they have it. If, on the other hand, I don't want someone to have that information, I will speak real fast and in a confusing tone. If I could speak for mankind, I would say that bright and intelligent people leave messages that are clear and easily followed. Anyone who doesn't is an idiot, moron or imbecile. Which one of these are you?

CHAPTER 49

LAUGHING OUT LOUD (LOL)

I am sick and tired of receiving text messages from you, and anyone else for that matter, with an LOL response. Everyone seems to use it without careful thought or consideration as to its meaning. If I send you a funny or amusing note, picture or link, your response is almost always the same – LOL. Really?! You literally laughed out loud? You found what I sent you to be so hysterical that you burst into laughter? For the record, I don't believe it. Not even for a second.

I think I have a decent sense of humor, but it is a rare event that something is so side-splitting funny that I would laugh out loud. I wouldn't suppress laughter, I would welcome it. It just doesn't happen like that with any great frequency. For you, on the other hand, everything is laugh out loud funny. You tell me that is the case because you write 'LOL' back to me all the time. Just so you know, I think you are a big fat liar. I think you just like writing 'LOL'. You obviously would not be a suitable test audience member for a new sitcom.

I am asking you, nicely, to please give the use of 'LOL' a rest for at least one month. I want to help you become more tolerant and selective of things that are funny. This will benefit you beyond your wildest dreams. Instead of sending 'LOL' return texts, you might want to reflect on how you really feel. If something is funny, isn't it entirely possible that you might smile or even chuckle a little bit to yourself? You may even experience a short HA! HA! Or HEE! HEE! That is about all that you

115

really ever do in the privacy of your phone and computer world. You do not LOL and you damn well know it.

Why don't we call what we do what it really is? Most of the time we see something as humorous with no real outward emotion. It is all internal. Rarely would anyone watching us ever really know that we found something amusing, unless we smiled or made some noise. The truth is that we are, more often than not, experiencing happiness inside of ourselves. We are laughing on the inside, not out loud.

So......we need to dispense with this LOL stuff. We need to be more honest in describing our true feelings. If I am laughing to myself on the inside, then I am LTM" ing...laughing to myself. I guess you can even chuckle to yourself (CTM) or even smirk to yourself (STM). If you just find something amusing, how about going with "Ha". If it is quite amusing, Ha, Ha, Ha (or Ha3). Is a Ha or LTM worse than an LOL? No. They are characterizations of truth. The recipient is not thinking, "oh my God, I did not get an LOL." I am so disappointed that they were only mildly amused. I am a failure in life. Trust me; that never happens.

The term LOL is tired, overworked and, for the most part, a flat-out lie. It is time for a change. I really think that people would be appreciative of the truth. Your jokes and theirs are not laugh out loud funny. They are just so-so. Big deal. Maybe all they deserve is a smiley face. What is wrong with a smiley face? Maybe you actually laughed internally. In that case, someone is entitled to an "LTM". We are all far better off doing a little LTM every once in a while, if that is, in fact, the truth. Go ahead and try it and then start letting others know you are doing it as well, and why. opefully, they are receptive to all of this and do not respond with a WTF. I hate that as well, unless, of course, it is not what it seems, and they can't respond right away because they are busy "Washing The Floor".

CHAPTER 50
WE NEED MORE FRUIT SEED TECHNOLOGY

I don't think I am alone in saying that I am ticked off with the seed people in their advances on fruit seed technology. They have made great strides with the watermelon. I am not sure where I would even find one with those huge black seeds. You know, the kind you spend hours flicking out of your fruit or storing in your mouth for spitting out in a can or in someone's face.

This change in watermelon/seed embodiment did not happen overnight. It was a gradual process. I am sure there are traditionalists who refused to eat seedless watermelon. They considered 'seedless eater's to be communists and wanted nothing to do with them. Times have changed to the point that it doesn't matter. Try and find a seeded watermelon. People who refused to get on the color TV bandwagon are in the same boat. Try and find one that is in black and white that is anywhere other than in a 3rd world country. I dare you.

But why did they stop at seed technology for watermelons? Why is it that you still have that white seed crap in cantaloupes? Why is it that you still find grapes with seeds and grapefruits with seeds? What is going on here? Who told the watermelon seedless society to stop with their pursuit of anti-spittoon excellence?

I can appreciate that maybe you need a little seedling of some sort in the fruit, so that you can grow more. That is probably why you find those little white things in seedless watermelon. I am not sure what the hell those are. They look like seeds, but they are squishy enough that you can eat them. Some people go through the hassle of picking them out.

117

I can't be bothered with that. Down the hatch they go.

There has to be a way to bring watermelon seedlessness to other fruits. Why isn't this front and center a national crisis and A-1 priority as it should be? I understand that some people like the seeds in their fruit. It makes them feel that they are dealing with the real McCoy. They are fools. Getting rid of seeds is a pain in the butt. To suggest otherwise is to argue for the sake of arguing.

I am calling on the US Department of Agriculture to fund a minimum of $1 Trillion to research this matter and find a solution. We waste plenty of money on lots of other things that are stupid and of little benefit to us. This seems like as good a waste as anything else. I am talking about doing something with worldwide consequences. I trust everyone sees this as well and will write their Congressmen to usher things along. At the very least, I hope I have planted the seed of a really great idea in your brain.

CHAPTER 51

MESSAGE TO NFL EXECUTIVES ABOUT HOME FIELD ADVANTAGE

Baseball is somewhat complex. It is almost like they have a rule for everything. The one rule that seems to make the most sense is the one that addresses 'home field advantage". It is universally known that any team that plays before its home crowd has an advantage over the opposition. The fact that the fans scream obscenities and boo the visiting team may have something to do with this. Nevertheless, it is obvious that playing at home makes a difference, which is why, in the game of baseball, the visiting team is extended the courtesy of batting first. This seems to make sense for a number of reasons; 1. It seems fair; and 2. If the home team is leading at the end of the top of the 9th inning, they don't have to play anymore, and, as a special bonus, the players can enjoy the rest of the day with friends and family.

With rare exceptions, teams almost always win more games on their home court or field. Even the Las Vegas odds-makers take this fact into consideration when determining the line on a given game. So, it would seem that, like baseball, all sports should attempt to approach the game with the same level of fairness. But they don't. Why do hockey games start with a dropped puck at center ice? Why do basketball games start with a tip off at center court? Is that fair? If the puck or ball were given to the opposition first, would that really make a difference in these sports? Probably not. It might make more sense to give the visitors a few extra goals or points at the beginning of the game. That should even things up.

119

I am waiting for the relevant commissioners to get back to me to see if this idea of mine is workable. I won't be holding my breath.

Football, on the other hand, is a totally different ballgame. Just like baseball, and unlike hockey, basketball or even soccer for that matter, there is always one team in football that always gets the opportunity to score first. Given the fact that the visiting team is subjected to a hostile crowd that is so noisy that players cannot hear quarterback signals, it is obvious that the home field advantage is huge. So how do they determine who gets the ball first in football? Do they have tall players gather at the 50-yard line and throw a ball up in the air to see who catches it? No! Does the visiting team get the ball first? Yes and No. What they do is they very generously give the visiting team the honor of calling a coin toss. Who developed this stupid rule?

It seems beyond strange that the visiting team should get the honor of calling the toss and that is the only courtesy that is extended to them in such a hostile environment. Why did some knucklehead come up with an idea the consequences of which are only 50/50? Since the powers that be recognized that home field advantage needed to be addressed, why did they come up with a stupid coin trick?

The correct solution is so obvious that one can only imagine that the people who came up with the coin flip idea were victims of a few too many shots to the head. Apparently, this was the best that their feeble minds could envision. Come on folks. This is just lunacy. What am I missing here? If you aren't going to automatically give the ball to the visiting team, then they should not be allowed to call the coin toss. That option is nothing short of an advantage in the form of an illegal gaming operation. Perhaps the captains of both teams should buck up for the right to make that call (best 2 out of 3). If that doesn't work, rock, paper, scissors should be considered as a suitable alternative.

And, by the way, since football is on my mind, I have one other thing about the game that makes me crazy. Why is it that some football announcers think that, when a team does get the ball, they are able to march down the field? I have looked at a great many football fields over my years and, although I have never personally taken a level to them, I am pretty certain that there is no part of a field that is higher or lower than the other. There is no upstairs and there is no downstairs to a football field. I think that is pretty much the case for soccer fields as well. When you have the ball, and go from one end of the field to the other, you move "across" the field. You do not "march".

Marching is typically associated with the military and high school or college bands. Marching requires movement in a synchronized fashion using a cohesive step routine. Obviously, there are some numb-nuts associated with football who do not seem to know the difference between marching and moving across the field. I guess that explains why they feel so strongly about throwing coins up in the air.

CHAPTER 52
WHEN IS NEXT THURSDAY?

When is next Thursday? I know you don't know. Why? Because you missed a freakin appointment; a really important one at that. How can that be? Such a simple question should never be subject to uncertainty. When you tell someone that you will see them next Thursday, you need to make sure that the two of you are on the same page. Obviously, that was not the case. I can't understand how, but apparently, that is exactly what happened. Because of your inability to appreciate proper date management you have caused embarrassment, unnecessary drama and all kinds of problems between us and with others. Therefore, I think it is critical that we get your lack of understanding on how to manage a calendar in check before you cause another world war.

Apparently, whatever date I would ascribe to next Thursday, someone who is not all that smart might beg to differ. You see, for them, like you, they think it is all a matter of perspective. If today is Monday, is next Thursday three days from now? You might say yes, but I hope you would have said no. Because if you said yes, you just proved my point about your total lack of understanding about the days of the week and how we schedule events between people. Just to be clear, three days from now is "THIS' Thursday. If it is THIS Thursday, it cannot also be NEXT Thursday. If THIS Thursday is 3 days from now, then NEXT Thursday is 10 days from now. THIS and NEXT are 2 different words. They have a different meaning. Get it?!!!

Now what if today is Friday. Is next Thursday 6 days from now? Nope. Six days from now is THIS Thursday or THIS COMING

Thursday. Next Thursday is 13 days from now. You see, there is always the concept of THIS and NEXT and you really need to keep that straight. Next week is the week after this one, but it could never occur during THIS week. If you buy into this train of thought, then you must also agree that NEXT Thursday can never be within the same week in which THIS Thursday is to occur. I know this all sounds childish, but, then again, we had that thing happen between us and I want to avoid it from ever happening again.

If this is confusing to you, I am not surprised. No less surprised than the stupid thing you did that caused me to write this all down in the first place. This is an obvious area where you seem to be lacking in basic logic and common sense. Since that is the case, I have a suggestion for you. If someone makes plans with you to do something THIS or NEXT any which day, do not assume you are in agreement. Assume you desperately need a clue and seek absolute confirmation. Do not leave anything to chance. The potential downside of a mistake can be huge. It can cause heartache, lost time and money. Given that fact, err on the side of caution. That should be the only error you make. One mistake is regrettable; doing it again is unforgivable THIS week, NEXT week and every week thereafter.

CHAPTER 53

WHAT DO YOU HAVE AGAINST TEA DRINKERS?

Isn't the taste and aroma of coffee the greatest thing since sliced bread? It can be mixed with almost anything. It makes for a great ice cream or even a flavoring to be mixed with milk.

Everybody needs their morning cup of Joe to get going and to satisfy that craving and urge. Starbucks, Dunkin Donuts, Seattle's Best and every breakfast place on this planet cater to the coffee drinker. You want a latte, you got it. You want French vanilla, hazelnut or Espresso; your wish is their command. Coffee is king and virtually every establishment pays homage to the lovers of coffee.

But guess what? Not everybody likes coffee. To some, it is a putrid and disgusting taste. Hard to imagine, but true. You are not going to believe this, but some people actually would prefer a nice cup of tea. For some people, tea serves the same purpose as a cup of coffee in the morning. It is not nearly as versatile (as I have yet to see a bowl of tea flavored ice cream) but it can be delicious either with nothing at all or with a little milk (or cream) and sugar.

There are some coffee drinkers who also like a cup of tea. Tea lovers hate these people. They are all over the place. Why can't they stick to their own kind? They like honey flavored, mint julep, peppermint, dandelion, rose petal and yummy tummy teas. That isn't tea and the people that make this junk need to go out of business. This stuff is liquid perfume for people who don't really like tea and want to say that they do.

124

They already have messed up coffee by creating zillions of variations. Now they want to do the same thing to tea. Forget about it. Step away from the tea counter and go about your business drinking your multitude of coffee flavors.

Why such anger about tea persecution? I will tell you. Imagine you are out dining at a nice restaurant. You have finished your meal and want a cup of tea to go with your fancy schmancy dessert. They bring you a beautiful teak box that is velvet-lined. Inside is the most awful assortment of tea flavors you could ever imagine. Who would like this stuff? Stupid coffee drinkers. Who puts this box together? Stupid coffee drinkers.

A real tea drinker will tell you (without even asking) that they like the basics or high-quality brands of tea. Many restaurants do not even have the basics. Why? Because they don't care about tea drinkers. To them, if you like tea, you are in the minority and your opinion is little appreciated. You should be thrilled that no expense was spared in buying a nice teak box. The contents are irrelevant.

So, you need to stop your insensitive behavior toward tea drinkers. Throw your teak box in the trash and stock up on some decent tea. Buy some for your home as well in case you have tea-drinking company. You already cater to the coffee drinker with your special brews. Now go the extra mile by thinking about the rest of the caffeine and decaf universe. If you are going to have tea, be respectable in your selection. What is respectable? How about a green tea and black tea? Not a pink tea or a minty tea. How about some of the teas that have been around for over 100 years, like Earl Grey and English Breakfast. How about some of the golden tea leaves that can cost up to $200 a cup? Now you are talking. Why are they these flavors so popular with tea drinkers? Because they are the real McCoy. If you wouldn't serve garbage to a coffee drinker, why would you present an inferior brew to a lover of tea?

Why don't all tea drinkers like the specialty stuff like coffee drinkers? If you are talking about the $10 to $20 a pound loose tea that you brew in various and assorted flavors from around the world, that stuff is awesome. But all of that other minty, boxed stuff is God-awful to a true tea drinker. It is called "foo-foo" tea. Not everyone calls it that name. But they should. Some people may like "Constant Comment", but, if you really are a lover of tea, constant comment is someone who needs to shut up. "Smooth Move" is definitely not a party favorite. It serves an ungodly purpose. You may as well put a stool softener on the table to everyone's delight. This insensitive and boorish behavior must stop once and for all.

It is high time that restaurants and coffee houses, and so-called friends and family, all of who don't give a rat's ass about tea loving beverage requirements, cease and desist from their discriminating behavior. The days of 10 canisters of different coffee blends and 1 for hot water are over. Remember the Boston Tea Party? You ain't seen nothing yet!

CHAPTER 54
NEW NAMES FOR BODY PIERCING

I was thinking the other day that, in this day and age, we have acronyms for everything. They have them in sports, they have them for texting and they have them for just about anything else you can imagine. And there is a good reason for it. We are just too busy to have to speak every word we want to say. We need to say things in as short a sentence and timeframe as possible, so we can move on to other things (also known as "MOTOT" …as in, I am done here. I need to MOTOT.")

So, the other day I was talking to a young lady who had one of those stud thingy's in her tongue. I could see it the few times she spoke since she was using acronyms for everything she said; especially when she would LOL. I could see her stud thingy with each of her "L's. But I digress.

So, what do we call the stud thingy in her tongue? A "tongue stud"? Please! You must be joking. I have come up with the perfect name.

A tongue stud shall now be known as a "TUD". And what about a "nose stud", what shall we call that? You guessed it, a "NUD". Get the picture? I can see an entire stud industry picking up on this. You will soon see ads for TUD and NUD combos for ½ price. Everyone will know what it means because it will soon be a part of our lexicon.

Am I done here? Hardly. Don't we have other parts of the body where studs are known to invade? How about belly buttons? What shall we call the button stud? If you are following my logic the answer is simple; the B-BUD (pronounced "beebud").

I really think I am onto something here. I am sure I have missed a few things and I will leave it up to my fellow citizens of the world to remedy anything I have left uncovered. I do have one other stud-related word for the ear. It is called: E-Stud. I confess that this does not sound as good as some of my other acronyms, but this is a work in progress. I have never liked the word 'earring' for an ear stud, because it is not a ring. Unlike a ring (which is round by the way), an earring must go through and all the way around an earlobe in the same way as a nose ring that goes through and all the way around a nose nostril. Nobody gives someone a set of diamond earrings these days that are true earrings. They are studs. They are giving diamond E-studs.

In this age of simplification, we need to step up to the plate and make sweeping changes, especially when they are so obvious and easily implemented. There will be some resistance at first by those who don't like to be told what to do, regardless of how practical or beneficial the result. But I am betting that my idea will catch on faster if it is not ascribed to me. Let someone else take credit. I will take pleasure in seeing it out there and popularly used. It will tickle my funny bone to hear someone acknowledge that someone has an awesome looking "NUD". Nothing will please me more.

CHAPTER 55

SEND YOUR OWN DAMN REGARDS

The other day I was speaking to a friend about a mutual acquaintance. Before we concluded our conversation, my friend asked me to send the acquaintance his regards the next time I saw him. Why do people do that? Why do they complicate life with these unnecessary obligations? I hear it all the time. "Tell them I said hi." "Tell them I extend my heartfelt condolences." "Tell them I was asking for them." I really have had it up to here with people who think I am their personal messenger. It is, quite literally, an unrequested imposition, and a rude one at that.

First and foremost, I think it goes without saying that, anyone who makes this request or demand of me is a lazy bastard. Instead of picking up the phone or texting or emailing this mutual acquaintance, they have decided to take an even easier way out by creating a burden that I could most definitely do without. The ease with which we are able to communicate with just about everyone these days is mind-boggling. Despite all that, people are continually trying to invent new ways to make it even simpler. I think that making things easy is a good thing, except when I get dragged into the process for no good reason.

And here is something that is probably not being seriously considered; once this obligation is created, what are the rules? Is there a timeframe for extending the regards that I have been asked to communicate? I would think that a week is a reasonable period of time to accomplish the mission. Two weeks is definitely pushing it. Within that time, I am required to make contact and let the mutual acquaintance know that regards have been sent. Even if I have no reason to speak to them, I have got to call or write and let it be known that good wishes are being extended by someone who is too lazy to do it without a hired messenger service. I would call and say, "Hi, how are you? Listen, I really have nothing important to discuss, but I want you to know that I was speaking to so and so the other day and they asked me to extend to you their regards. You have their regards now, so I guess I have fulfilled my obligation. You can decide to do what you wish with these regards, but please do not ask me to send them yours."

And what if you call me during the time period before I complete my mission and ask me if I have finished the job? Should I feel guilty for not having done so in what you consider to be a timely manner? What if I decide to refuse the job and tell you "I am sorry, but I am not your errand boy. If you have something to say to our friend, do it yourself?" Is that socially inappropriate? Also, what if I accepted the mission and then changed my mind along the way? Should I call you and tell you that I have decided that the obligation is too great, or I am a lazy bastard as well and just cannot bear the stress of handling an obligation of such considerable magnitude? Is it okay for me to hire a proxy? Can I give the proxy the regards that you gave me and then have them give them to the person to whom they were ultimately intended?

Now that you have me obsessing about all of this, I have another bone to pick with you. It makes me crazy when people like you ask me to send their regards to a mutual acquaintance in the form of "telling them I was asking for them." Tell them I was asking for them to do what? Nobody ever bothers to ask this question in response to this unwelcome request. We just smile and go along with the conversation without skipping a beat. But we need to be honest with ourselves. We really have no idea what the hell you are talking about when you make this statement. It is an incomplete sentence. "Tell them I was asking for them to check out the new TV Guide? Tell them I was asking for them to go to the grocery store and buy a cooked chicken? How about speaking proper English for a change!

As much as I hate you asking me to send your regards, there is something else I want to bring to your attention. I cannot remember the last time you asked me if your regards were properly sent. I guess that means that you hold your own regards in low regard. If that is the case, then I am thinking this through way too much and should just ignore your request in the first place.

A SPECIAL REQUEST FROM ME TO YOU

Thank you for reading my stress relieving diatribe. I hope I did a good job getting your points across. If it accomplished even the slightest benefit for you, I was successful in my effort. After all, there has to be at least one topic I covered that is a constant source of your own personal aggravation. I may not have said it as well as you might have, but I am sure that certain someone will catch my drift.

Maybe there are even some situations I have described that have now become new sources of irritation to you. Whereas they may have been minor inconveniences to you in the past, you now see them as hugely problematic and I have upped your stress level and anxiety. For that I can only say "my pleasure, we aim to please".

Obviously, there is only so much I can cover all at once. I am compiling lists of new topics virtually every day. Perhaps you have thought of a few others that came to mind while reading this material. Surely you have some pet peeves that have been bugging the heck out of you. You can continue to allow them to fester within you, or you can do something about them.

If I missed a topic that is near and dear to your heart and you would like to get it out there, I will be happy to rant on your behalf. Please login to "welborneiler.com" and send me a message. I will consider the best way to voice your displeasure. All suggestions and what I do with them become my property. But you really shouldn't care about any of that. Especially if I have unburdened you and let that special someone have it "loud and clear". In fact, you should pay me for helping you out. I am glad to be of service. :)

WE

ACKNOWLEDGEMENT

I would like to personally and thankfully acknowledge my dear friends and loved ones who helped in recommending ideas and organizing this assembly of negativity. Some of you did way more than others. Some of you didn't do a damn thing. Most of you did it unwittingly. You should all be content in the knowledge that I recognize your contribution and I am thanking you here without calling out anyone specifically by name. You know who you are, and if you need me to mention you by name, you have an ego problem that will be dealt with in my next book.

I would also like to thank all the family members, friends and strangers who have crossed my path in life. I appreciate all the happy moments that we have shared. I also appreciate the great many annoyances and countless hours of aggravation you have provided as material for inclusion in my writings. I am hoping for and looking forward to you continuing to be rude, annoying, and discourteous. No need to stop now. I know I can count on you to give me an infinite array of tidbits I can write about for my own amusement and, perhaps, the benefit of others. Please don't disappoint me. I know that you won't.

ABOUT THE AUTHOR

Welborn Eiler is a licensed business professional residing in New England, where he has lived all his life He also owns a design company that he developed for some of his other creative pursuits. He likes all sports and especially certain musical groups and movies that begin with the letter "A". He also likes beef, chicken and fish and is likely to choose any of them in a response card for a formal event. Welborn is not immune to conducting himself in an annoying manner and neither confirms or denies that his family and friends give rise to fodder for his writings.

Welborn Eiler has taken the first step in amassing a collection of material that is solely designed to tell someone off with absolutely no consequences whatsoever to anyone but him. Having spent decades helping people and businesses navigate their problems, he brings his warped sense of humor and brutal honesty to others to help resolve problems and open a dialogue and discourse on what he hopes to be some very interesting conversation. This is only the beginning. The worst is yet to come.

Did I miss one of your pet peeves? Visit me at "www. welborneiler.com" and send me a message with the details. You never know when I will strike again.